RECYCLING

JEROME GOLDSTEIN

RECYCLING

HOW TO REUSE WASTES IN HOME, INDUSTRY, AND SOCIETY

SCHOCKEN BOOKS ● NEW YORK

First published by Schocken Books 1979
10 9 8 7 6 5 4 3 2   80 81 82

First Edition

Copyright © 1979 by Jerome Goldstein

Library of Congress Cataloging in Publication Data
Goldstein, Jerome, 1931–
    Recycling.
    Includes index.
    1. Recycling (Waste, etc.) I. Title.
TD794.5.G64   333.7   78-20983

Manufactured in the United States of America

Contents

Acknowledgments

Any form of recycling takes a great deal of cooperation. So did this book about recycling. My special thanks to a good friend and colleague for many years, Maury Franz, who contributed the chapter on "The Smallest and Best Recycling Center—Your Own Compost Heap," and to Nora Goldstein for contributions throughout the book, plus her chapter on "Mandatory Deposit Legislation and Recycling." The recycling experiences, insights, and personal resources of such persons as Pete Grogan, Kevin Mulligan, Richard Tichenor, Wayne Davis, Wesley Hamilton, Clarence Golueke, Steve Suleski, and Mildred Lalik were particularly helpful.

JEROME GOLDSTEIN
NOVEMBER 1978

Introduction

Garbage consists of the leftovers from meals, paper, and plastic cartons, ranging from orange peels and lettuce leaves to the morning newspaper.

Garbage is a "bunch of junk," anything you don't want: bottles and cans, plastic toys, old tires, sofas, rubber tires, junked automobiles.

While persons have different viewpoints on what garbage is, cities and public health officials have tried to standardize the definition. To them, garbage is a fraction of the solid wastes that must eventually be treated by the city. It has many different sources and qualities, and varies by season and area.

Officially, *garbage* "is the animal and vegetable waste resulting from the handling, preparation, cooking, and serving of foods." It originates primarily in home kitchens, hotels, and other places where food is stored, prepared, or served.

Sludge consists of the solids produced after sewage is processed at the local wastewater treatment plant. Each person in the United

States with access to a flush toilet produces about 100 gallons of sewage daily, which in turn yields about 0.2 pounds of sludge.

Sludge comes in several different grades—raw, digested, or activated—depending on the treatment process. The daily total of sludge produced in the nation comes to 15,000 dry tons, and the figure will double within the next 10 years.

Raw or primary sludge is the first product of the sedimentation process which takes place at the wastewater plant. It is extremely high in moisture content, foul-smelling, and biologically unstable. After digestion, the material is dark gray to black, has an odor suggestive of tar, is readily dewatered, and has solids that are somewhat granular in texture.

———

Refuse comprises all of the solid wastes of the community, coming from homes, institutions, industry, and agriculture. It includes garbage, rubbish, ashes, dead animals, bulky wastes, abandoned cars, demolition wastes, and sewage treatment residues.

Refuse includes the organic: paper, garbage, rags, grass clippings, leaves, wood, yard trimmings, sludge.

Refuse also includes the inorganic: metals, tin cans, stones, glass, bottles, other mineral refuse.

———

In the United States, the per capita production of solid wastes (all categories listed above) increased from 2.75 pounds per day in 1920 to more than 6 pounds per day now. Studies show that the rate of production in many areas is actually closer to 20 pounds per person per day. No one knows for sure whether or not the 2 billion tons of manure produced at feedlots, or wastes generated at canneries, paper mills, pharmaceutical plants, etc., are counted in someplace along the line. But the piles are real, whether figured in the data or not.

Because of the tremendous pressures to purify our nation's air and water resources, and because of the lack of room at the old dumping sites, sludge and garbage are front-page news as one city after another faces up to the crisis.

Untreated and unrecycled, these wastes haunt us by causing health and pest problems—a blight to our land, water, air, and selves. They also cost each and every one of us astronomical amounts of tax dollars.

Not until the last few years have most city governments even admitted having a problem with solid-waste disposal. The approach has been to spread refuse around and hope it would not be noticed. This policy, of course, never was right—but, at least for the most part, it succeeded. Few noticed or complained about the spreading dumps, and the fish did not write nasty letters to city hall.

Fortunately or unfortunately, depending on your viewpoint, those days are gone forever!

The only choice we have is to recycle our wastes. And that is what this book is about:

> Recycling in your home and in your yard, garden, or farm;
> Recycling in your neighborhood;
> Recycling by your city;
> Recycling by businesses.

By its very nature, there are many facets to recycling. For many, recycling provides a way to live harmoniously with the limited resources of the world, and to safeguard those resources for the future. For many, recycling makes sense on the most pragmatic terms—a way to produce energy from wastes and to renew dwindling resources. Economists are at last joining environmentalists on the road to recycling. And even investors are finding the early entrepreneurs in recycling businesses more attractive.

Public support is vital to successful recycling programs. ECOZ used this parade float to rally the citizens of Zelienople, Pennsylvania, to climb aboard the recycling bandwagon.

1

Breaking the Garbage Can Addiction

A friend in Maine got fed up with peeling plastic from every fresh-food package from bananas and tomatoes to meat and potatoes. She began to shop where foods were not always tightly presealed—where she could carry home food, not nondegradable packaging. She spent more time in farmers' markets and mom-and-pop food stores and far less in supermarkets. More bread was purchased in the local bakery, and even more was baked right in her own kitchen. To save time, she bought a food processor. As less of the so-called fast and convenient foods were taken into her home, far less packaging junk had to leave in the garbage cans. There was an inverse ratio between the amount of whole foods she cooked and the trash she had to put out twice weekly.

Our friend in Maine is by no means unique in understanding that the best way to reduce waste is not to buy it in the first place. In varying degrees, millions of Americans have developed a recycling ethic that is economically, morally, socially, and environmentally sound. Even better, it's fun, healthy (invariably junk food comes with the most junk packaging), and relaxing (haven't you ever had to rush out at midnight when you heard the garbage truck down the street?).

A University of Kentucky professor and his family combined purchasing policies with their throwaway philosophy to develop a program that they called *Modern Living without Garbage Service.* "One day in June 1971," recalls Wayne Davis, "my wife asked the garbage collection men to take the smelly old cans with them and said we just don't want to be bothered with garbage and trash anymore."

The Davis family, like almost all the rest of us, had been thoroughly addicted to garbage cans. Their household regularly filled two large cans twice weekly, and the entire routine of stinking cans, swarms of flies, and raiding animals was accepted as part of the way of life in modern society. The thought of getting away from it all was pleasing, but Professor Davis "was afraid that after a short effort at handling our own garbage, we'd sheepishly request service to resume."

But after some years he proudly pronounces the venture to be a success, offering this explanation for why they did it and how the system works:

> One consideration was money. The several dollars per month we paid for garbage and trash collection may seem a small part of a budget, but it's considerably more than we pay for our daily newspaper. Stopping it was a logical step in our savings efforts to reduce nonessential services such as professional haircuts and hiring a plumber to fix a leaky faucet.
>
> The most important factor, however, was a desire to find an alternative to what I consider a self-destructive lifestyle that grew out of our "use it once and throw it away" economic philosophy.
>
> Today our system works like this: newspapers, glass, aluminum, cans, and pasteboard go to our recycling center, which is open just one day each month. Magazines go to hospital waiting rooms. Kitchen garbage is buried in the garden.
>
> Here is a rundown of our procedure: In the kitchen we now

have two garbage sacks. One holds both glass and cans, which we separate at the recycling center. We rinse, remove labels from, and flatten the cans. Our second sack is fitted inside a plastic garbage basket with a folded newspaper beneath it. Into it go all kitchen scraps. When it fills, I take it to the garden and bury the contents— bag, newspaper, and all.

Since both bags fill slowly, little work is involved in handling them. Cans and glass are carried out about every two or three weeks and the kitchen scraps about weekly. If the garbage begins to stink, my wife simply closes the top of the bag. This contains the odor and is a signal for me to remove the bag.

Putting garbage into the garden has never caused serious problems. Directions for composting say not to use grease or meat scraps because they attract dogs and rats. With my unfenced yard, I found dogs would dig up the garbage. At first I countered this problem by covering each site with stones. Then I discovered that a single old tire is satisfactory. After a burial site has been covered for a week it's no longer attractive to dogs, so I just move the tire when I bury the next bag.

When the ground is frozen, I bury the garbage under a pile of leaves where the ground is always soft. In the hot summer, when our garbage is entirely vegetable matter unattractive to dogs, I simply throw it between the corn rows and cover it with the grass clippings my neighbors put out for the trash collector.

Buried garbage decomposes quickly. It's attractive to earthworms and other invertebrate soil conditioners. After three or four weeks nothing can be found of the garbage except scraps of eggshells and chicken bones; even these disappear with more time. My garbage has been a welcome addition to the leaves and manure which I used to turn a plot of clay from my basement excavation into a fine garden with excellent soil texture and fertility.

There are disadvantages to our system. Preparing cans and jars for recycling is extra work. The extra bags to separate garbage, trash, and cans and jars are a nuisance. Some of our garage space is needed to store materials between trips to the recycling center. However, we consider our effort a success. I doubt if we'll ever go back to garbage cans and collection service.

A great many special interests—packaging manufacturers, national beer and soft-drink companies, "Big Brand" food purveyors, and an unusually large number of politicians—are quick to say that they would be most willing to use less packaging, refillable containers, etc., but they cannot, because "the American consumer demands convenience." Simply and plainly, that defense is *hogwash!*

Right now, there is a significant minority of Americans who go out of their way to recycle and buy less trash. They seek out beverages sold in returnable bottles; they separate bottles, cans, papers, and organic wastes; they transport them to recycling centers or place them in separate containers for pickup. That minority—when supported by local ordinances or statewide legislation—can quickly become a majority, as is evident in the following specific cases:

PUBLIC RESPONSE TO VERMONT'S DEPOSIT LAW

"By all measures, public support of the deposit law in Vermont is strong, and is growing with experience," declares Congressman James M. Jeffords. The legislated deposit system is relatively simple. A deposit of at least five cents is required on each beer and soda container sold in the state, to be refunded when the container is returned to the store. Stores are required to accept containers of the size and type they sell, but are allowed to limit hours of redemption. The beverage distributors, who pick up the containers from the retailers, are required to reimburse retailers for their handling costs at a standard rate of 20 percent of the amount of the deposit.

The bill passed initially by a slim margin in 1972, attempts to repeal it were rejected by a larger margin in 1973, and the law was strengthened by an overwhelming vote in 1975. Observes Representative Jeffords in a report on the Vermont experience co-authored by Donald Webster, "The momentum clearly lies with those who want the legislation to be strong and effective, and most observers feel there will be little resistance to strengthening amendments proposed for the 1978 session."

Students were the backbone of the Zelienople recycling effort when it started in 1971. This glass smasher exemplifies the available technology when the project began.

From a twice-a-month collection effort that included aluminum cans (here, about to be flattened), the program is now countywide with estimated recycled volume reaching 10,000 tons in 1979.

(photo by Ray J. Thompson)

In 1975, an opinion poll of 800 adults by the *Burlington Free Press* showed that nearly 70 percent of Vermonters supported the deposit law. A mail survey sent by Jeffords later that year to 10,000 state residents indicated that 78.1 percent felt that Congress should pass national legislation "similar to Vermont's." In 1977, the question was repeated in a similar survey, and the support had grown to 93 percent.

Representative Jeffords and Mr. Webster, who is director of Vermont's Environmental Conservation Agency, conclude:

> There is no question that support for the state deposit law is strong, and is growing with experience. People have grown accustomed to it, and they like it. The return rate for empty containers has grown from an initial level of 83 percent to more than 95 percent, and beverage sales in the state are booming. Politicians running for office talk about improving and strengthening the deposit law, but never about repealing it.
>
> In a state populated primarily by thrifty Yankees who believe in commonsense solutions to problems with minimal government interference, this is probably the strongest possible evidence that the law is working well. As any knowledgeable Vermont political observer will testify, the law could not have obtained its widespread popularity if it had been causing the problems which opponents insist would be brought on by deposit legislation, or if the benefits were not visible, tangible, and significant.

ZELIENOPLE—WHERE VOLUNTEER RECYCLING BECAME PUBLIC POLICY

Immediately following Earth Day in 1970, thousands of volunteer organizations across the country set up recycling centers. Most of these flourished for several months or several years, but then faltered under the problems of variable markets, transportation costs, and storage facilities. The spirit of recycling was high, but the realities of volunteers facing a full-time task were harsh.

The town of Zelienople, Pennsylvania—located just north of Pittsburgh—is one of a handful in the U.S. which has seen its recycling program move from a volunteer program managed by environmental activists to a publicly supported program still spurred on by environmental activists who, simultaneously, are politically astute. Attorney Wesley Hamilton is the founder and president of ECOZ (Ecologically Concerned of Zelienople, Inc.), the group that developed the twice-a-month collection effort in 1971 which became a countywide system in 1978. ECOZ demonstrates how recycling can move from the latent stage to the overt.

Two years ago, with the help of the Butler County commissioners and the Western Pennsylvania Conservancy, ECOZ purchased a 150-acre tract to construct a permanent recycling center. Influencing positively a number of environmental concerns, the site also has a wilderness area that ECOZ is preserving as a natural park, complete with nature trails and a stream for public use. The purchase price of $70,000 was financed by the Conservancy, with the county commissioners guaranteeing the mortgage.

ECOZ then constructed its first 6,000-square-foot structure and storage area to recover wastes, and the county agreed to provide CETA (Comprehensive Employment Training Act) positions to operate the program during the week, with volunteers handling the facility on weekends. According to Hamilton, "initial problems in the early stages were a general lack of public acceptance of recycling concepts and the need for a processing facility, a general lack of public education concerning the need for recycling, and the consensus that recycling was just a fad."

But that first year of operation in 1976 indicated the depth of public concern—771 tons of material was recycled, compared to the previous year's 172 tons. The system is classified as a user-delivery system, in which the residential patrons deliver their recyclable commodities (cans, bottles, papers) to the ECOZ plant site, while a selected number of commercial and industrial places are served by an ECOZ truck. ECOZ also acts as a transfer station for materials collected by independent recycling groups in the area.

In 1977, Hamilton and his colleagues built a second plant to process scrap tires and broken industrial wooden pallets, and to provide for community leaf collection and composting. Butler County, acting as an agent for ECOZ, received a demonstration grant from the Pennsylvania Department of Environmental Resources for $89,000 for that plant. ECOZ realized a 64-percent growth in its recyclable volume, shipping 1,260 tons.

In 1978, ECOZ took a quantum leap forward when Butler County received a $1,223,000 grant from the state's Department of Environmental Resources for construction of a countywide system to be fully owned and operated by ECOZ. Hamilton explains the success this way:

> The countywide system is founded on the belief that voluntary recycling and low-technology resource-recovery systems are solutions to solid-waste disposal problems in contrast to a high-technology system which is environmentally inefficient and financially extravagant for a rural population, as exists in Butler County. We are building 20 small drop-site buildings where residents can bring their recyclable materials. The drop sites will be open five days per week and operated by CETA personnel. It is estimated that our volume will dramatically increase during the next five years, and we estimate 2,500 tons for 1978, and 10,000 tons for 1979. ... By drawing together state monies in the form of grant assistance, federal monies under CETA, the municipalities providing land, the County of Butler providing expertise, and the private sector giving of its time and effort, we have truly evolved a community project.

ACHIEVING RECYCLING GOALS IN SANTA BARBARA°

The Santa Barbara Resource Recovery Program is a community-based, countywide project, jointly sponsored by Santa Barbara

°This information is excerpted from reports presented at the Second Annual California Recycling Conference sponsored by the California Resource Recovery Association. The complete *Proceedings* of the conference were published by the Community Environmental Council, Inc., P.O. Box 448, Santa Barbara, CA 93102.

and the Community Environmental Council (CEC), a private, nonprofit educational organization. In 1974, CEC members distributed leaflets at the entrance to the county transfer station, asking residents to place unsegregated scrap metal (washing machines, water heaters, etc.) in a designated place where local scrap dealers could pick it up after bidding. This project netted the Santa Barbara community more than $25,000 in the first year. That same year, residents and groups were urged to bring newspapers to bins on selected days, and the proceeds were used to rent a warehouse. "At this point," explains CEC co-director Hal Conklin, "we were recovering 5 percent of Santa Barbara's newsprint; our goal was 50 percent."

To reach that figure, CEC carefully developed its own "pyramid strategy," in Conklin's words, "taking one element at a time and making it work smoothly and economically." After securing contracts with a paper company that sells recycled newsprint, CEC increased its volume by offering to credit various charities and causes for paper brought to the center. In this way, paper recovery was built to 25 percent. The CEC encouraged participation by the business sector when it offered to pick up and pay for computer cards, computer paper, and office ledger paper.

Next, newspaper curbside pickup routes were created in certain areas, and then expanded. Conklin further explains:

> Because of this service, neighbors are encouraging each other to save newspapers and other recyclables (which they bring to the center). The result is that we are now recovering 50 percent of the 55 tons of newsprint that is delivered into our community each week, making us one of the largest newspaper recycling programs in California.

The Santa Barbara Recycling Center serves about 140,000 people, and based on annual figures, recovers about 4,000 tons from the waste stream.

Initiatives by the Private Sector

The Paper Stock Committee of the American Paper Institute, in a report entitled "How To Recycle Wastepaper," establishes basic guidelines for citizens, municipalities, retail businesses, and offices to recycle their wastepaper.

Here they point out, for example, that used corrugated boxes are the largest single source of wastepaper for recycling. As many retail stores, supermarkets, factories, and department stores have an abundance of corrugated boxes, the report shows how businesses can profit from the sale of used corrugated by establishing a used-corrugated collection program.

> A northeast region of the A&P supermarket chain reports that 110 stores in the area generate some 250 tons of corrugated containers per week. The corrugated is either backhauled to warehouses or sold directly to dealers. The savings in trash-hauling fees alone is close to $2 million per year for the region.

The Paper Stock Committee suggests following the guidelines listed below to recycle corrugated boxes successfully:

Step 1. Establish a market for your wastepaper. "The first step in any recycling effort is to determine the market value of the paper your company generates."

Step 2. Keep used corrugated separate from the trash, free of contaminants like plastics, metal objects, plastic- and wax-coated cartons, and junk like floor sweepings, wood, food waste, cans, trash, etc.

Step 3. Devise an efficient handling system.

> The system might be nothing more than tying up the empty boxes with cord and piling them in the backroom or outside the back door. Stores generating greater amounts of corrugated might require the installation of a small baler, which can effectively reduce the amount of storage space required.

Retail stores that are part of a chain of stores often find it more profitable to backhaul used boxes from individual stores to regional warehouse facilities for processing, rather than handle the material on a store-by-store basis. Large balers or compactors are installed at these central processing points to handle the combined tonnage of used corrugated generated in the region.

Step 4. Arrange for pickup of your corrugated. If the quantity of used corrugated is large enough, often the wastepaper dealer will pick it up. For smaller retailers or businesses, local residents with trucks may pick it up free of charge and deliver it to the wastepaper dealer, keeping the profits.

Step 5. Establish a relationship with local dealers: "By doing so, you will guarantee a relatively stable and reliable outlet for your collected paper."

The report emphasizes that the primary motive for businessmen to establish recycling programs is economics:

> The Northern Division of the Food Fair supermarket chain, for example, is realizing savings in disposal costs, as well as profits from the sale of the used boxes generated by the division's 275 stores. The chain estimates a monthly savings of $300 per store, or $82,500 per month for the entire region. In addition, the chain receives up to $80,000 per month by selling its baled corrugated to recycling mills. The recycling program, therefore, represents some $1.9 million annually for the Northern Division.

J.C. Penney and Sears stores and various plants of the Morton Frozen Food Company are just a few of the department stores, factories, and assembly plants throughout the country which have established recycling programs. "A midwestern glass company once paid $300 per month for disposal of its used corrugated, but now earns $800 per month by selling the corrugated to local paper stock companies." By viewing wastepaper as a valuable raw material to be recovered, the committee concludes, businesses can turn wastes into profits.

RECYCLING HIGH-GRADE OFFICE PAPERS

The Paper Stock Committee report also outlines a program for recycling high-grade office wastepaper. They point out that "high-grades account for approximately 20 percent of all wastepaper utilized by the recycling industry as a raw material, and are more valuable in the marketplace than most other types of wastepaper because they can be used as a substitute for woodpulp in the paper-making process."

The committee demonstrates the effect that an office recycling program would have on urban areas, since most office buildings are located in urban settings:

> The EPA estimates that 90 percent of all office waste by weight is wastepaper, which ends up in already crowded landfills. . . . effective office recycling programs can have a significant impact on reducing the volume of solid waste disposed of in municipal landfills.

The following procedures are offered as guidelines.for establishing a recycling program in an office building:

Step 1. Establish a market for your paper.

Step 2. Announce the program to employees.

Step 3. Separate recyclable papers at the desk.

Step 4. Devise an efficient collection system.

Step 5. Keep wastepaper free of contaminants. The following are recyclable materials: white typing paper, white writing paper, white photocopy, white scratch paper, tabulating cards, index cards, and computer printout paper. The following are contaminants: envelopes, carbon paper, other sensitized paper, blueprint paper, film photographs, Scotch tape or glue, metal objects, spiral binders, fasteners (staples are acceptable), newspapers, cardboard, magazines, books, all colored paper, file folders, junk.

Step 6. Publicity and follow-up on the program.

A living example of a large-scale high-grade wastepaper recycling program can be found at one of the world's largest office complexes—the World Trade Center. The program is operated by the Port Authority of New York and New Jersey, which operates the World Trade Center in lower Manhattan. The Paper Stock Committee reports that the program was started in 1974. "Today, the program has become an accepted part of the daily routine of nearly 10,000 employees in the 'Twin Towers' and includes almost 75 private companies and various federal and state governmental offices.

"The Port Authority recovers several grades of wastepaper, totaling approximately one ton per day. The largest single grade is manila tabulating cards, traditionally one of the most valuable grades for recycling."

The income accrued from the program more than offsets the expenses needed for the operations, demonstrating how offices might profit financially by recycling their wastepaper. Expenses to get the program under way were approximately $1,500, current labor costs are about $1,700 per month, and the Port Authority is planning on purchasing an additional $1,000 worth of equipment.

Even More People Recycle When It's Mandatory

While it's true that many Americans willingly recycle when dropoff sites and curbside pickups are available, the fact is that many are not so willing. In November 1977, for example, a community phone book and paper recycling drive was conducted in the Denver, Colorado, area. Mountain Bell (telephone company) of Colorado provided financial and staff aid; Eco-Cycle of Boulder, a well-organized recycling group led by Pete Grogan, provided expertise in setting up dropoff points and arranging pickups; a local supermarket chain offered use of its parking lot facilities; civic and government organizations gave their official blessings to the drive. Multimedia publicity was arranged, including newspapers, radio, and stuffers in telephone company bills. The governor endorsed the effort, proclaiming that every effort would be made to recycle all the old directories at the statehouse.

Instead of being a waste-disposal problem, the old phone books and paper could become a resource material for a developing cellulose insulation manufacturing industry. The money from the sale of paper to insulation manufacturers would then be used in other recycling projects in Colorado.

The potential of the recycling drive was described as "enormous," but the reality of the effort was far less. Public participation in the volunteer effort never really materialized. Sponsors of the drive hoped to collect about 2,500 tons of old phone books; instead, only about 70 tons were turned in to recycling centers. Pete Grogan of Eco-Cycle said that the poor response was because people are "just not used to recycling. ...We Americans grew up with the attitude of throwing everything away."

Thus breaking the garbage can addiction can and does run into great difficulty when performed on a voluntary basis. That's why *mandatory* source separation is being advocated. Richard Tichenor, who directs an organization in New England called Recycling and Conservation, Inc., described the experiences of Nottingham, New Hampshire, with a mandatory source separation recycling system. As explained in a following chapter, average compliance of Nottingham residents ranged from 85 to 97 percent.

For families like the Wayne Davis household in Kentucky, personal commitment is enough to break away from the garbage can addiction. Certainly impressive amounts of materials are recycled on a voluntary basis. But Nottingham, New Hampshire's, 95-percent compliance is the kind of achievement that requires some kind of mandatory system.

How we move from a hit-or-miss recycling basis to full-scale recovery will undoubtedly take education—and then some firm legal steps and broad-based incentives. Last year, for example, Los Angeles spent a modest $10,000 to promote a recycling program to 10,000 households which volunteered to separate their garbage before pickup. The city hopes to pay for the program through sale of recycled materials.

Next, there needs to be a reduction in garbage collection fees to those individuals who put out less garbage than their neighbors for public collection, or none at all! That idea has been in fact proposed in New York City by the general counsel for the city's Environmental Protection Administration. Suggested William Friedmann:

> With landfill space diminishing and restrictions on incineration, one of the most serious environmental problems facing society today is the elimination of garbage. Using an income-tax deduction or credit suggests a partial answer in defusing this solid-waste time bomb.
>
> Alternatives to present disposal techniques for our ever-increasing supply of garbage (25,000 tons per day is the current figure for New York City) must be fostered by material incentives to individuals, not just by appeals to our environmental patriotism or conscience. Unfortunately, experience has shown that incentives lacking material support do not motivate the vast majority of us to do anything.
>
> Source control and recycling are major alternatives to current disposal techniques. Programs banning disposable bottles and containers, etc., have some limiting effect on the garbage supply at the source. The recycling of our garbage is also a means of controlling our garbage supply. Recycling, however, requires encouraging the uninterested to engage in source separation (separating recyclables—glass, metals, paper, etc., from organic garbage) at home and at work.
>
> A tax deduction or credit program could be implemented through a tax certification from a qualifying organization containing a stated dollar value, that you delivered either at your curb or at a collection point your separated recyclable waste material. This would encourage reduction in the quantity and mix of our garbage

and eliminate matter which would complicate recycling processes such as garbage conversion to energy and composting.

In one case we know of, the Oakland, California, City Council finally decided to exempt Terry Seaborn from an ordinance which charged all residents for garbage pickups. Seaborn recycled his papers and glass, composted garbage in his backyard, and took plastic four times a year to the landfill. Commented Seaborn after his struggle to set a precedent: "People have to feel they can do things for themselves."

Throughout our nation's history, very little pollution has been abated without legislation or litigation or the threat of such action. Dumping and burning wastes—wastes that need to be channeled into renewable resources—must be viewed as a major cause of pollution. When wastes are dumped into our rivers and oceans, pure water becomes only a figment of a technologist's imagination. When wastes are dumped onto our land, our soil suffers, our groundwater supplies are threatened, and our nation's scenic beauty is desecrated. When wastes are burned into the air, our health is directly imperiled. In short, the garbage can addiction is making our lives miserable! And costing us billions besides!

The recycling solution—and the support—begin at home.

2

Recycling Centers
Start at Home

When citizens work together, they are able to make a tremendous impact on complicated municipal problems, and waste recycling is a prime example. In the following examples of successful recycling programs in neighborhoods and cities around the country, the basic feature is source separation. That is, each cooperating household *separates* its wastes into such categories as glass, paper, and metals. The collector—whether voluntary, private, or public—can then channel the materials into the various markets for recovery. For many reasons, source separation is the preferred method for moving America from a throwaway society to a recycling one. The critical issue is how to increase citizen participation in source-separation programs.

The Eco-Cycle Way*

Eco-Cycle is not yet a household name throughout Colorado, but the way it's growing it soon will be! Founded in Boulder in July

---

*The following information about Eco-Cycle of Boulder, Colorado, is based on material supplied by Pete Grogan, who, with Roy Young, serves as co-director.

ECO·CYCLE

ACCEPTS THESE ITEMS:

PLEASE SEPARATE and Have At Curbside by 9 am
On Scheduled Saturdays.*

Corrugated Cardboard
Flattened and Tied.
(NO light cardboard)

Glass Bottles, Jars and Containers— All Kinds & Colors

Do Not Break.
Remove Lids, Rings, Foil.
(NO pyrex, mirrors, ceramics, light bulbs, window glass)

Aluminum Beverage Cans, Foil, Food Containers

Steel Beverage Cans, Bottle Tops, Small Metals

Tin Food Cans Flattened

Clean. Remove BOTH Ends From Can.
Place Ends Inside Can. Flatten
With Heel of Hand, Shoe, or Hammer.

Automobile Parts and Scrap Metal

(Mufflers, Engine Blocks,
Batteries, Radiators,
License Plates, Copper, Pipes,
Metal Furniture, Doors, Windows)

Used Oil
Place in
Plastic Containers
with Screw-On Tops.

Tires

For More Information Call 444·6634

*In case of heavy snow or rain on the scheduled
collection date, pickup will be the next day (Sunday).
Tune to KADE Radio 1190 AM for further information.

Eco-Cycle used this simple leaflet to instruct Boulder area residents about how to
prepare materials prior to collection.

of 1976, Eco-Cycle, a nonprofit recycling company, is presently collecting 15 percent of that city's recyclable waste. Eco-Cycle is a comprehensive recycling program that collects newspapers, high-quality paper, corrugated cardboard, glass containers, tires, motor oil, appliances, and steel and aluminum cans. In two years the program has expanded into seven Colorado communities and Rocky Mountain National Park. The Eco-Cycle masterplan includes a Denver and Colorado Springs metropolitan recycling system. All major population areas would have curbside collection of recyclables; all rural areas would be serviced by dropoff locations.

Presently, the collection system relies on the participation of community organizations. Community organizations from church groups to high school clubs, civic groups, and Scouts sign up for an opportunity to collect recyclables. These organizations are paid for providing a one-day labor force. It's an excellent fundraising activity for the groups and it's ready-made. They don't need to publicize it, spend money on organizing it, bake cakes, etc. They just need to arrive at 8:00 A.M. on a Saturday with 20 members willing to move 40 tons of recyclables.

Eco-Cycle currently uses at least four community organizations each Saturday. Because of the overwhelming response, organizations now have to sign up eight months in advance. After two years of operations, one thing is certain: the collection system works. At the inception of the program, the idea of using volunteer organizations on a rotating basis was laughed at by political figures in the community. "You can't build a program using volunteers"; "They won't show up"; "They'll be unreliable," Eco-Cycle was told. Neither the City of Boulder nor Boulder County was excited about supporting such a program. But 700 angry concerned citizens attended one city council meeting and convinced them that Eco-Cycle, was a workable solution to a serious problem.

For Eco-Cycle, the community organizations are an inexpensive labor force. The sale of the recyclable materials collected

Old school buses, used as collection vehicles by Eco-Cycle, are found to be safer for use with youth groups, can be purchased inexpensively, and hold just as many recyclables as a truck.

would not earn enough money to pay 20 full-time laborers, the drivers, and the expense of running and maintaining the collection vehicles. This system is also Eco-Cycle's way of giving something back to the community by supporting community organizations. For example, one high school band outfitted the entire band with new uniforms with Eco-Cycle proceeds.

The Eco-Cycle collection system is superior to traditional newspaper drives. First, the rotation of organizations allows each organization to participate as often or as little as it cares to. No organization is responsible for the every-week collection. Second, newspaper drives were primarily fundraising activities; thus, they were only designed to collect easy-to-sell materials. Usually, materials such as motor oil, cardboard, and tin cans were ignored. Eco-Cycle provides for all of the marketing, as well as collection

vehicles, drivers, insurance, collection bins, storage locations, publicity, and supervisors. This all adds up to a regular, reliable collection service for residents of the community. For the first year of operation, each household was provided with a once-a-month service; after the first year, service was increased to twice a month.

The community responds to this system because it is very simple for them to get involved. All they have to do is place their recyclables curbside in front of their homes. All materials are collected every two weeks, so it's a matter of saving the material and remembering the collection day. The collection system is also much more energy efficient than having everyone drive a car full of recyclables to a dropoff center.

As outlined above, the Eco-Cycle collection system for source-separated recyclables works extremely well. However, problems arise in the areas of marketing and equipment acquisition.

Markets for recyclables must exist; the purchaser must be interested in materials generated by recycling programs; they must have a high demand for these materials; and they must be in a location in close proximity to the program. Eco-Cycle is in a "recycling desert" with respect to the marketing of recyclable materials. The state of Colorado has only one glass-container manufacturer, making the demand for glass in the area very small. Colorado has only one small paper mill whose present demand for recyclable materials is met without Eco-Cycle supplies. The only steel mill in the area does not purchase small loads of scrap cans (small loads are less than 20 rail cars a month). The major purchasers of recyclable materials are located near the East and West coasts. Current rail rates do not allow Eco-Cycle to be competitive on either coast. For example, scrap glass (cullet) costs $50.00 per ton to transport from Denver to Los Angeles. Upon arrival in Los Angeles the cullet can only be sold for $30.00, making it economically unfeasible for the Eco-Cycle program to ship glass for recycling.

Unfortunately, the situation is the same for shipping other recyclable materials.

When U.S. paper prices plummet, as they did in the summer of 1978, recyclers on the coast export their paper to countries like Brazil, Japan, and Korea. Eco-Cycle does not have the capability of selling paper overseas because of the long distance to a port.

Price fluctuations are also a difficult problem. Paper prices have dropped overnight from $60.00 per ton to zero. Paper contracts with guaranteed floor prices are difficult to obtain because of the nature of the business. There is hope that in years to come, prices will stabilize because of increased demand brought about by increased prices for virgin materials.

There is an old saying in the recycling business: "Recyclables are bought and not sold." This couldn't be more true. The purchasers call recyclers when they need materials; when they don't, there is no concern for recyclers.

As for equipment, Eco-Cycle uses two-ton trucks and old school buses for collection vehicles. School buses are safer for use with youth groups, they can be purchased relatively inexpensively, they hold just as many recyclables as a truck, and they can be heated and lighted during bad weather or late days. Eco-Cycle presently uses 11 school buses with seats removed to get the job done. A used baler was purchased to bale cardboard and corrugated cardboard. This baler produces mill-size bales which are loaded by a forklift onto rail cars and sold to mills throughout the West when prices allow. An appliance tin-can crusher is presently under construction. Roll-off trucks are used to transport the nearly 40 tons of glass collected each week. This service is rendered by a local trash company. The necessary roll-off trucking equipment will cost the program over $100,000. The key to successful recycling is handling the materials as few times as possible. Cans should be collected, then shredded or baled, then loaded into roll-off containers which are dumped into a rail car. A roll-off truck and containers are a must for transporting recyclables. Many of the costs of the necessary recycling equipment are prohibitive. For this reason, Eco-Cycle played a major role in the development of the Colorado Recycling Cooperative Association.

The Colorado Recycling Cooperative Association (CRCA) has as its members all of the comprehensive recycling organizations in the state. The CRCA plans to share equipment and to market materials cooperatively. Thus, instead of each program's purchasing roll-off equipment at $100,000, the equipment will be purchased by the cooperative and shared by all projects.

The CRCA cooperatively markets some materials. Presently, all cans are sold through the statewide cooperative. Thus, a rail carload of cans might have cans from three members' recycling projects. A prospective buyer of newsprint needing 500 tons of wastepaper could contract with CRCA for the paper. CRCA will request a premium price for the paper and will be able to attain it for filling the necessary demand. No individual project would be capable of filling the order.

Beyond the marketing and equipment needs, one of the largest obstacles recycling has to overcome is the public's attitudinal problem. Recycling programs are attempting to change deeply ingrained human behavior. The "throw-it-away" syndrome is presently quite normal behavior, even though it is wasteful. As a nation, we are involved in an energy crisis and a raw-material shortage problem. We import virtually 100 percent of certain metals, and then turn around and throw 75 percent of them away after one consumer use. We are paying higher prices for those cans and bottles that carry our consumer products than ever before. We are polluting our land, water, and air with our solid waste. Selling recycling to the public is extremely difficult. Selling toothpaste is simpler: a manufacturer can promise cleaner, whiter, fresher teeth and possibly fewer cavities. A recycling program can only promise very indirect benefits: energy savings, a cleaner environment, etc.

Eco-Cycle has used bumper stickers, T-shirts, door-to-door flyers, newsletters, radio and television advertising, milk-carton advertising, city water bills, electric company bills, newspaper articles and advertising, church bulletins, and a calendar to publicize its program. Today 25 percent of the households in Boulder recycle. Eco-Cycle's director feels that 50 percent is an obtainable goal.

As for funding, Eco-Cycle has received assistance from the U.S. Environmental Protection Agency Office of Solid Waste, the Denver Regional Council of Governments, the City of Boulder, Boulder County, and the local Department of Labor CETA program. The Environmental Protection Agency (EPA) funds were for a demonstration project. Eco-Cycle's co-director, Pete Grogan, wants the program to be self-sustaining as soon as possible: "To design a recycling system that is dependent on volunteers and subsidies is to design a failure. We will do more harm to the recycling field than good with a program that needs federal funds every year. Asking for initial seed money from the federal government is justified because we are nonprofit and are working on a solution to a serious 'national environmental problem.'"

Grogan is opposed to high-technology resource-recovery systems. He feels they are highly energy dependent; they demand high quantities of trash with no consideration given to waste reduction and conservation. They do not create jobs, they destroy resources. Most of all, they aren't working, and the public taxpayer is suffering the biggest loss. Grogan met with President Carter's energy officials in an effort to persuade them to stop high-technology programs. "Carter's energy staff looks at source separation recycling as Mickey Mouse programs; they think recyclers still have little red wagons. They love high-tech systems; all they can see is the fuel output and they actually think they are producing energy from nothing."

Eco-Cycle plans to enter into the production phases of recycling. "We have no real desire to be in the manufacturing business, but because of a lack of markets and because of the way we have been treated by the markets that do exist, we really have no choice," Grogan stated. The first such project will be a local storefront. The storefront will sell repaired appliances such as refrigerators, stoves, washing machines, toasters, televisions, and lawn mowers. Eco-Cycle receives hundreds of broken appliances a month. "I found out what built-in obsolescence was real quickly; half of the appliances we receive look like they left the showroom last week. I never had any idea how many major appliances were dumped until we started recycling them," says Katie Kelley of Eco-Cycle, who maintains that the only thing American technology has perfected is obsolescence.

Until August 1978, all the appliances were sold to scrap dealers. Now many are reincarnated. The store will also sell recycled brands of paper and oil, composted potting soil, and a wide variety of recycled materials to the public. Eco-Cycle plans to operate a bottle-washing facility similar to the one developed by the Portland (Oregon) Recycling Team. The plant washes bottles collected by the recycling program and sells them back to the users. This program will create increased energy savings and at the same time create new markets. Eco-Cycle is presently in the research phase of this project.

Eco-Cycle plans to enter into one area of the paper-processing field. Egg cartons and grocery sacks are presently being explored, but no definite plans are set. Also, Eco-Cycle is interested in working with the Colorado State Highway Department on a rubber-asphalt tire-recycling program. The Arizona Transportation Department has been building highways with used tires for the past 11 years. In addition, Eco-Cycle is considering a waste-oil recycling program.

> With the present collection system, a 20-city program, our own processing and trucking equipment, and the manufacturing facilities, not only will recycling work, but community organizations will be paid well and thousands of well-paying job opportunities will open up in all stages of the operation.

Grogan feels that many metropolitan areas have attempted to solve their solid-waste problem with high-technology garbage monsters, but no large metropolitan area has ever attempted a total source-separation, low-technology approach. As he says, "The solution to the problem is quite simple. With 6 percent of the nation unemployed, let's put them to work processing resources." On a metro-scale, the program will generate enough material not only to interest purchasers, but also to interest some of them in moving processing facilities into the area.

Presently, two of Eco-Cycle's programs are in the Denver suburbs. One more Denver suburb is considering an Eco-Cycle proposal. Grogan feels that given the proper equipment, 40 percent of the Denver area's trash (wasted resources) could be collected and recycled, and that sooner or later a solution will be implemented because landfill space is running out and resources are becoming scarce. While recycling is not the total solution to the problem, a combination of such techniques will minimize waste. Waste-reduction programs will be necessary; more reuse of materials and recycling may have to become mandatory and be enforced by law: "I would prefer to see it happen voluntarily, but time is running out."

A major national educational effort is needed. People are not going to just wake up tomorrow morning and begin recycling. The Department of Commerce, the Environmental Protection Agency, and the Department of Health, Education and Welfare should all now be working on a major resource-education program. The millions of dollars being used to construct high-technology resource-recovery plants could be put to better use by implementing source-separation programs and providing recycling education.

Following Pages: Comprehensive recycling is the Eco-Cycle philosophy; hence collected materials include mountains of cardboard, tires, glass cullet, and barrels of cans.
(photos by Allen Price)

Materials Accepted by Eco-Cycle for Recycling

The Eco-Cycle philosophy is comprehensive recycling; many organizations recycle only those materials that are financially profitable. Eco-Cycle believes in collecting almost all possible recyclable or reusable materials. In this way a wide variety of materials are saved and put back to use. Eco-Cycle collects the following types of materials:

Newspapers: Newsprint is the single largest volume of materials collected and recycled. Almost every home receives at least one newspaper; in Boulder alone, Eco-Cycle collects 200 tons of newspapers per month. This paper is sold to de-inking plants that produce new newsprint and to cellulose-insulation manufacturers who produce home insulation.

High-Quality Paper: High-quality papers, including computer printouts, tabulating cards, and white and colored ledger paper, are collected from office complexes such as city and county offices, police offices, banks, etc. This paper is sold to paper mills that produce new high-grade paper.

Corrugated Cardboard: Eco-Cycle receives corrugated cardboard in the form of used box containers from homeowners and businesses. This material is baled and sold to paper mills. New paper and paperboard products of every kind are manufactured from this material.

Glass: Eco-Cycle collects all types of glass containers for recycling; these containers are used in the manufacturing of new glass containers.

Tires: Tires are collected and segregated for recappable carcasses and still usable tread. These are sold to tire recappers. Damaged or previously recapped tires are presently being stockpiled for a future asphalt-rubber road-building project.

Motor Oil: Used motor oil is collected from homeowners and stored in holding tanks. The oil is sold to waste-oil processors who filter and refine the oil.

Appliances: Major and minor appliances are collected. Most of these appliances are sold for scrap metal; others are repaired.

Radios and Televisions: These items are scrapped for parts and are being repaired on an experimental basis.

Clothing: This is the newest material collected by Eco-Cycle. Old clothing and rags are used in the manufacturing of diverse products and materials.

Ferrous Scrap Metals: Ferrous scrap metals constitute approximately 7 percent of the municipal solid waste (excluding automobiles). About 50 percent of the ferrous fraction is steel cans. Eco-Cycle collects all types of cans. The straight steel cans (with a tin coating) are sold to the steel industry; bi-metal (aluminum and steel) beverage cans are sold to the copper precipitation industry.

Eco-Cycle also collects all forms of scrap metal, including doors, screens, engine blocks, lawn mowers, appliances, camper shells, and autos. These materials are repaired and put back to work whenever it is economically possible. All nonrepairable materials are sold to scrap dealers.

The Nottingham Experience*

Source separation is basic to the many small, voluntary recycling efforts throughout the country. It also accounts for most of the resource recovery in this country, according to the U.S. Environmental Protection Agency's *Third Report to Congress on Resource Recovery and Waste Reduction.* Nevertheless, making source separation an integral part of official town disposal systems has generally been regarded as impractical. Successful preliminary experiments with a small number of households and specially designed separation containers during 1971 caused researchers at Recycling and Conservation, Inc., to question this assumed imprac-

---

*Richard Tichenor is the director of an organization called Recycling and Conservation, Inc. His responsibilities have involved him deeply in the resource-recovery efforts of Nottingham, New Hampshire. The material which appears below is based on two reports by Tichenor in the magazine *Compost Science/Land Utilization—Journal of Waste Recycling.*

ticality, and, together with subsequent research on volume-reduction techniques, convinced them that the workability and economic viability of small-scale systems should be tested by means of a functioning system. As a result, Recycling and Conservation, Inc., entered into a joint project with the small town of Nottingham, New Hampshire.

The Nottingham system serves the predominantly rural town of Nottingham, New Hampshire, which has a year-round population of approximately 1,200 people and an additional summer population estimated to average several thousand. It replaced a town dump where residents brought their solid waste to be disposed of by open dump burning, which became illegal as of July 1, 1975. Subsequent to several educational meetings and other efforts within the community to inform the residents of how the system would work if it were adopted, the system was voted in as the official town disposal system at a special town meeting.

Under the Nottingham system, residents still bring their solid waste to the old dump site, but they are no longer bringing a heterogeneous mess to be burned in a manner that pollutes the air, results in leachate in the groundwater, and attracts rodents. Rather, they are bringing separated resources, raw material for the future production of economic goods, and a segregated residual which is burned in a small, environmentally acceptable incinerator. Instead of a burning dump, the facility receiving the materials is a 30-foot by 60-foot wooden building equipped with volume-reduction equipment for the recycled materials and the incinerator for the nonrecycled materials.

The system actually begins in the homes of the residents. Solid waste is not accepted at the town facility unless it is separated into designated categories, bottles and cans are rinsed out, and metal rings and caps removed from bottles. The category designations for ordinary day-to-day household waste are newspaper, corrugated cardboard, clean mixed paper, metal, glass, and rubbish. (Large, infrequently disposed of items such as appliances, scrap iron, brush, etc., tend to be segregated naturally.) The simplest way for the residents to accomplish the required segregation of materials which are normally mixed is to have separate containers or containers with separate compartments for each category.

All paper categories are presented at one window of the plant, metal and glass at another, and rubbish at a third. Brush, appliances, scrap iron, and other such items are piled outside in designated areas.

UNDERLYING CONCEPTS

The Nottingham system represents an application of some general concepts to the particular circumstances of a given town. The principal concepts underlying the system are as follows:

1. *If a resource recovery system is to be successful, it must afford some direct net economic benefits to the community employing it. In a small town this may be possible with a system of home separation and low-technology volume reduction.* Unfortunately, many of the benefits of resource recovery—the reduced rate of depletion of natural resources, energy savings from using recycled materials instead of virgin materials, etc.—are not strong inducements for individual communities to engage in resource recovery because these benefits accrue to individuals and groups outside the community and/or to society as a whole. In the terminology of economists, they are "external benefits" or "positive externalities." Even though they benefit as members of the larger society, most communities recognize that their share of the very small contribution that their individual effort can make to the social benefits will be minimal. Since the financial situation of most local governments does not permit altruism, they accept or reject resource recovery on its economic merits as a disposal system. In short, it must be economically competitive with the disposal alternatives available to them. As discussed above, this is not likely,

at least in small towns, if heterogeneous materials are mixed together, but home separation eliminates very costly aspects of resource recovery. It does not, however, alter another fact which can be a problem for a small town. Most small towns are likely to be far enough from markets for some or all of the recycled materials that some volume reduction will be required to make shipments to market economic.

2. *Home separation should be a legal requirement enacted by the vote of an informed citizenry.* Allowing participation in the resource-recovery part of a town's disposal system to be an individual option is clearly not cost effective. If recovery is the least-cost method for "disposing" of a given material, quantities of that material in the pure disposal stream increase costs unnecessarily. In addition, many people who would support mandatory home separation may not participate in an optional program because they have no assurance that overall participation will be sufficient to lower costs enough to make their own effort worthwhile. Of course, a mandatory system must have widespread support and should not be attempted without putting it to a vote of the people. That the electorate should be "informed" goes without saying, but it is made explicit here to emphasize the importance of public informational and educational efforts prior to the vote. Voters should fully understand home-separation procedures so they do not expect them to be either more or less demanding than is actually the case.

3. *The decision as to what materials and how many categories of materials should be recycled must strike a balance between maximizing economic rewards and minimizing householder problems.* While the "costs" (time, effort, etc.) to the householder of segregating various materials are difficult, if not impossible, to quantify, they must be considered. Pressing for separation that is too difficult or involves too many categories can cause noncompliance and/or costs in excess of benefits. Too little segregation reduces the revenue from recycling, leaves too many resources to be burned or buried, and increases disposal costs.

PUBLIC PARTICIPATION IN NOTTINGHAM

Skeptics doubt that large percentages of people in a given community will, in fact, alter their lifestyles to throw different components of their waste stream into different containers. Low participation in voluntary source-separation programs throughout the country is taken as an indication of a basic resistance to source separation. Implicitly, if not explicitly, it is often assumed that this resistance will be reflected in mandatory systems in the form of noncompliance. There are, however, reasons to believe that many people who would not participate in a program which is a voluntary, ad hoc, adjunct to the regular disposal system *will support and comply with procedures which are an integral and mandatory part of their community's official disposal system.* The prima facie evidence from New Hampshire systems which have fully integrated source-separation recycling tends to support that belief. Estimated participation rates in the systems which are voluntary are on the high end of ranges usually cited for more ad hoc voluntary programs. More significantly, estimated compliance rates in the mandatory systems are quite high in absolute terms.

The average compliance over a 12-month study period was 95 percent for recyclables viewed as a single category. However, the corresponding percentages for the individual categories ranged from 97.3 percent for glass to 85 percent for newspaper, with metal compliance falling between the other two materials at 93.2 percent.

One factor believed to be of considerable importance is the manner in which the ordinance was enacted. It was not decreed by town officials, but rather adopted, with the support of town officials, by a public vote. This vote was preceded by an educational-information campaign which included meetings and mailings explaining the proposed system and separation procedures. The support of town officials, the educational effort, and the public vote are all believed to be quite important.

Educational-information efforts also continued after the system and mandatory separation received a favorable vote. This was particularly true during the period when the plant was under construction and during the first six months of operation. There was also one mailing in the second year of operation, and one mailing in the third year. These latter two mailings updated residents on how the system was working, and provided them with telephone numbers which they could call if they had further questions. These "postadoption" efforts are also thought to have contributed to the high compliance rate, although there is no way of knowing if they were required to reach the levels achieved.

Another factor which may have contributed to the high compliance rate is the fact that compartmentalized waste containers were made available to any household wanting them. Specialized

Collection vehicles operated by Downey, California, were used to collect 1,300 tons of recycled materials—newsprint, glass, and cans—in 1978.

containers are not thought to be essential. Each household can devise its own methods for maintaining the segregation of materials. Nevertheless, between 50 and 60 percent of the year-round households did take advantage of this opportunity, and the fact that a ready-made system was available probably had a positive psychological impact as well. It demonstrated one way in which segregation could be maintained, and removed the potential objection that residents were being told what to do but not how it could be done. The stackable containers chosen by most households also demonstrated that it could be done without devoting additional floor space to waste containers.

In short, Recycling and Conservation, Inc., believes that programs undertaken to increase public understanding and acceptance are the basis of high compliance. However, this is not to say that these same programs would have achieved participation in a voluntary program comparable to the compliance with the mandatory program, but rather that a mandatory ordinance achieved through and supported by a good educational-information program is probably the key to successful source-separation recycling.

The DART Program in Downey

After a year and a half of study and interaction with volunteer group and industry representatives, in May 1975 the city council of Downey, California, authorized its Department of Public Works "to prepare contract documents related to the collection and processing of recyclable material from single-family residences." The program to promote and implement source recycling in Downey came to be known as DART—"Downey At-home Recycling Test." At the start, mixed newsprint, glass, and cans were collected from 1,600 homes.

By November 1976 the test program was considered a success, collections were expanded citywide, and the acronym was changed to signify the "Downey At-home Recycling Team." In February 1977, in an effort to stimulate participation, the Glass Packaging

To stimulate citizen participation, these senior citizen volunteers assembled and mailed descriptive literature about DART—"Downey At-home Recycling Test." The campaign worked extremely well.

Institute engaged a public relations firm (Burson-Marsteller) to review the program and recommend a new promotional effort. It included a citywide mailing of a DART packet with a message from Mayor Hazel Scotto, instructions for recycling, and a new DART identification strip. Local newspaper articles and school programs also carried the message. The immediate result was an increase in volume to 123 tons per month.

In 1978 Downey recycled 1,300 tons of material, although, explains Robert DeSio, superintendent of physical services in Downey,

> the cost of handling is still greater than the revenue. In an attempt to cut cost, the rubbish company will now be picking up the recycling material every other week, a change from every week. . . . We have had good community acceptance and support

of the program, and are exploring ways for business, industry, and large apartment buildings to become involved.... California has a new law that will soon be in effect that will increase a city's dump fee 25 cents if the city has no recycling program. With the new scheduling and fee change, we are hoping to be in a more financially practical position next year.

Recycling in Davis, California

In 1972 a few volunteers launched the Davis recycling effort by forming the Resource Awareness Committee of Davis (RACD) and getting permission from the University of California at Davis to set up a recycling center on campus property in the downtown area. The center received glass, aluminum, bimetal cans, and newsprint. Commodity buyers and secondary-materials dealers hauled the materials away.

In July 1974 the Davis City Council passed an ordinance requiring the separation of newspapers from garbage, and arranged with the Davis Waste Removal Company (DWR) to collect the separated papers at the curb along with the garbage. DWR used a separate scooter for newspaper collection only. Explains DWR president Charles Hart:

> We handle approximately 125 tons per month of recyclables: 85 tons of newsprint, 35 tons of glass, 4 tons of bimetal cans, and 1 ton of aluminum. This represents about 10 percent of the garbage that we collect each month. Roughly two-thirds of the recycled materials are collected by our employee, while the other one-third is brought in by the public. For that material which we collect, the only requirement is that recyclables must be placed at the curb in shopping bags on regular garbage collection days. It is not necessary for the homeowner to wash out containers, crush cans, break glass, or even sort by material. We have tried to make the participation as simple as possible, and we think that a good 40 to 50 percent of the households do recycle at least some of their waste each month.

(photo by Nugent, Courier-Journal and Louisville Times)

The pilot project in Portland, known as the ORE Plan,
represents the beginnings of an alternative to present
garbage collection and disposal methods.

Specially designed racks under standard collection
vehicles enable crews efficiently to transport newspapers which residents keep separate from kitchen
garbage.

On the subject of the economics—profitability—of recycling, we find that we presently sell about $3,000 worth of recyclables each month (gross income), while operating expenses consume about $3,000 per month: one scooter and a full-time employee to go house to house; five drop boxes for storing and hauling recyclables to market ($15,000 investment); amortization of can-crusher ($2,000 investment); trucking of recyclables to market (two full truck-days per month at $320 per truck-day); minimum one hour per day of management time to keep the center clean and check on routes; daily garbage service (two two-cubic-yard bins full of trash are emptied at $250 per month).

Thus, we do not consider recycling to be truly profitable. Nevertheless, to be breaking even with recycling after all of these years of losing money is indeed encouraging.

Unfortunately, we have no control over the market price paid for recyclables, and our gross income from recyclables could just as well be $1,000 per month as $3,000 (if newsprint again dropped to $2 per ton), while our recycling expenses stay at $3,000 per month. Recycling will then be a drain on our business again, and when our total waste operations start losing money, we will have no choice but to go to the city council for a rate increase. Because the council has ordered us to recycle as a part of our contract with the city, the council must be prepared to make up the deficit through the rate structure by which we are compensated.

. . . We feel that recycling is important in making the public conscious of its waste, and hope that through this awareness the public will waste less. Although this line of reasoning—coming from a garbage company—may surprise you, it is our conviction that recycling is an integral part of professional waste management, and we consider ourselves professionals.

Recycling Operations in Other Communities

INNOVATIVE COLLECTING IN MADISON AND PORTLAND

Beginning in September 1968, the city of Madison, Wisconsin, began a newspaper salvage project which is still in operation today. According to Edwin Duszynski, director of public works at the time, original publicity to rouse public support centered around doorknob hangers distributed to some 20,000 households. "We had newspaper display advertisements which were run at no cost by the newspaper," he recalls. "Naturally, there were many newspaper stories. There were free radio announcements, TV programs, and spots."

The design and construction of special racks underneath collection vehicles were important to the success of the project. The rack holds a cubic yard of paper when full; rubber ropes fastened to the vehicle prevent newspaper bundles from falling out. Back in 1970, the racks cost the city $100 in material and $70 in labor. Extra collection time is minimal. If the paper rack fills up before the truck fills with refuse, dump trucks are located in the area for unloading paper. At the end of the day, one of the collection men drives the paper-filled truck to the salvage dealer.

Citizen cooperation in the municipally run newspaper recycling project has been extremely high.

PORTLAND, OREGON

Richard Duncan, a systems science professor at Portland State University, and others devised a low-cost, employment-intensive garbage collection and recycling service called the "ORE Plan." As in other curbside plans described, recyclable materials are separated by householders; then small-sized vehicles are used to pick up *both* recyclable wastes and mixed garbage at *one visit*. Collection fees provide the main base, which is supplemented by income from the sale of secondary materials.

The first business to implement the ORE Plan was Cloudburst Recycling, Inc., which served a community area of 5,000 households. A small truck acted as a "satellite vehicle" to a large van truck parked in the neighborhood where materials were temporarily stored, thus reducing collection costs. In the initial month of operation, an estimated 2,800 pounds of wastes was collected from

80 households, of which more than 50 percent by weight was recycled.

While the ORE Plan must be categorized as an experimental concept, it nevertheless represents the beginnings of an alternative to present municipal garbage-collection methods—perhaps one that will be taken seriously in areas that are most prone to implementing the tax limits of California's Proposition 13.

MARBLEHEAD AND SOMERVILLE, MASSACHUSETTS

In 1975, two Massachusetts communities, Marblehead (suburban) and Somerville (urban) received grants from the Environmental Protection Agency to demonstrate the effectiveness of large-scale materials recovery in a communitywide weekly multimaterial curbside collection program. Paper, cans, and glass were to be collected.

According to Penelope M. Hansen, EPA project manager, Marblehead has recovered from 23 to 33 percent of its residential solid waste stream each month since the program began. Somerville has recycled from 7 to 10 percent. The public education efforts which brought about the high level of participation in Marblehead were rated as well planned and extensive. An affluent suburban community of 23,000, Marblehead had an effective recycling effort well before the EPA project. In contrast, Somerville—a densely populated urban community of 90,000—had no previous recycling experience.

The EPA program provided for three levels of separation: all flat paper; clear glass and cans; and brown and green glass, and cans. All recyclable materials were collected weekly in a compartmentalized vehicle.

Other communities where recycling efforts have penetrated the waste stream have been described in Chapter 1. In each case, their success can be traced to a single individual or small group with ability to rouse the public and the politicians, and to pull all the loose ends together. Even then, the "War on Waste" is one battle after another.

Children's playgrounds, such as this one located on a former landfill, can be made from recycled lumber and other "trash that never was."

3

Things to Make from Trash That "Never Was"

To the innovative person, the Robinson Crusoe-type who has the knack of "making do" with bits and pieces of miscellaneous items, recycling means utilization far more than it implies source separation and resource recovery. By using your imagination and creativity, someone's junk can become your gold. In the home, the garden, the community, and your lifestyle in general, there are countless items to make from trash that "never was."

Home gardeners have performed an amazing number of such simple adaptations—old tires that become planters when filled with topsoil and planted with tomatoes or strawberries; Styrofoam coffee cups which, when a hole is poked in the bottom, serve as seed starters; plastic jugs, with the bottoms removed, that provide protection against late frosts for plants set out in spring; old wooden windows that serve as parts for a greenhouse or cold frame.

In a recent issue of a magazine called *Humanizing City Life* (formerly *Doing It*), an article called "How to Recycle Almost Everything" cited such examples as "Polyunsaturated shoe polish (vegetable oil gone bad? Good, use it to put a shine on your shoes).

The skins from just-peeled bananas will turn the same trick."

Recycling by adaptation has become increasingly practiced—in the home, kitchen, workshop; outside in the garden and yard; and also in the marketplace—flea markets, garage sales, auctions, etc., where recycling simply means selling (or buying) items which someone else might put out for the trashman. In some cases, the exchange is conducted at barter fairs.

Recycling 'Cycles

The children who live near Ben Billings in the outskirts of Denver, Colorado, have come to appreciate his knack for recycling old bicycles. Ben makes regular trips to the Eco-Cycle storage area in nearby Boulder, where the operators put aside thrown-out bicycles for him to salvage from them as many spare parts as he can. By a combination of mixing and matching, *voilà!* A "new" bicycle is available for a neighborhood child.

In Everett, Washington, Chester Whalen is another person who likes to work with what he calls "pure junk which nobody would steal." According to him, "the only way you can't fix a bike is if it's been wrecked good by a car. You just need to put a little work into it and take your time." Over a winter, Mr. Whelan pieces together about 60 bikes and now sells them at a weekly flea market near Everett for $15 to $20 each.

Other Recycling Ideas

Publications like *Mother Earth News, Whole Earth Catalog, Rain, Horticulture, Harrowsmith, Popular Mechanics, New Age, Country Journal, Alternative Sources of Energy,* Garden Way books, and many others carry reports regularly about how people make pre- and postdiscarded materials useful. Here are some examples:

Railroad Ties: For building raised beds for planting; terracing and a number of landscaping objectives. An Arkansas gardener built a simple vertical wall for his greenhouse by sinking two used railroad ties (costing $4 each) about 30 inches into the ground.

Human Hair from Beauty Shops: If you make a practice of cutting your children's hair at home, or have a friend who is a barber, and you also happen to have a problem with deer munching on your fruit trees in your home orchard, then you should try making some "hair bags." From the *Orange County* (New York) *Farm News,* published by the area Cooperative Extension Service, comes this advice on controlling deer browsing in the young fruit orchard: Collect human hair from local barbershops or beauty parlors, and place it in any type of weather-resistant bag. Nylon stockings or plastic open-mesh produce bags work fine. Then, hang the hair bag in the tree to be protected. The size of the hair bunch need not be any larger than a softball. In some orchards, hanging the bags in trees in the first few rows adjacent to the woodlot is enough to discourage the deer browsing. If you've got a severe browsing problem (and access to enough barbershops), hang a bag in every tree. Says county agent Warren Smith: "We offer no guarantee, but it seems to be working for some growers."

Old Telephone Books: Tear them into bits and use as basic stock for papier-mâché.

Wood Clothespins: These make unusual dolls when faces are painted on the tops and cloth-scrap clothing is added.

Rug Making: A tip from *The Swiss Family Robinson* illustrates the range of how-to-do-it techniques:

> We leveled the floors first with clay; then spread gravel mixed with melted gypsum over that, producing a smooth, hard surface, which did very well for most of the apartments; but I was ambitious on having one or two carpets and set about making a kind of one in the following way:
>
> I spread out a large piece of sailcloth, and covered it equally all over with a strong liquid, made of glue and isinglass, which

This rabbit pen was reconstructed from an old chicken coop found on a farm. All that had to be bought was the wire meshing.

The children's wagon was built from part of the door frame torn out when a house was redesigned. "When I look for old lumber," says Bob Ayers, "there is such an abundance that I can get the best of the crop."

saturated it thoroughly. On it we then laid wool and hair from the sheep and goats, which had been carefully cleaned and prepared, and rolled and beat it until it adhered tolerably smoothly to the cloth. Finally it became, when perfectly dry, a covering for the floor of our sitting room by no means to be despised.

Glass Jugs and Milk Cartons: Old gallon jugs can be used as mini-greenhouses to protect plants. A simple way to remove the bottom from glass bottles is to tie a heavy string soaked in gasoline or lighter fluid around the bottom of the jug. Light the string, and when the jug becomes sufficiently heated, plunge it into cold water. In the process, the bottom will drop off. Other gardeners convert empty milk cartons into frost protectors by cutting out their bottoms. The cartons are placed over plants and thrust about one inch into the soil so as not to blow over. Tops can be folded open during the day to allow ventilation, and then closed again on colder nights.

Child's Playground from Tires and Miscellaneous Lumber: Let your imagination go as you devise your own "jungle gym" for your children and grandchildren. (Speaking of children, there are all kinds of toys and dolls to be made from old clothing and "junk.")

THE ART OF RECYCLING WOOD

Of the many once-used substances lying around, one of the easiest to reuse is wood. Constructing toys, sheds, dining room tables, or rabbit pens from old wood does not require heavy machinery and is relatively inexpensive if a good source can be located. Bob Ayers in Emmaus, Pennsylvania, is one such person who combines his hobby of building things with the availability of low-cost, "recycled" lumber.

Over the past few years, Bob's projects have included transforming a chicken pen into a rabbit pen, building a garden shed, and designing and constructing a toy wagon. Much of the wood used for these projects was found either in old piles at the lumberyard, at renovation sites of old wooden structures, or at the scrap yard.

"Wood is the ideal material to work with," said Ayers:

> You can find good-sized pieces of wood or wooden beams once part of an old farmhouse. Even if there are nail holes or blighted sections, you just cut between the holes, working with the wood's problems. When I go out to look for old lumber, there is usually such an abundance that I can get the best of the crop.
>
> Because wood becomes harder with age, it is also a very durable substance with which to reconstruct things. Even if you have to invest in a sander and stripping materials, using old wood is still cheaper in the long run. We went to a scrap yard and found wooden beams, 3½ inches by 6 inches and about 10 feet long for $1.50 apiece.

Ayers reconstructed his rabbit pen from an old chicken coop he found on a farm. All he needed to do was to buy about five feet square of wire meshing. The shingles for the roof were obtained at no cost from scraps at a nearby lumber mill. The children's wagon was built from part of the door frame torn out when redesigning his house. A garden shed is made from aluminum siding found at the scrap yard which was added onto an existing base.

When working with recycled wood, however, Ayers feels there are a few basic ground rules. "It helps to be somewhat of a handyman, a person who likes to design and at least sand and treat the wood. Also, finding good sources of recycled wood requires a knowledge of the local area—where the scrap yards and lumber mills are located or where renovation projects are being done. Finally, try to have storage space to build up an inventory of supplies."

Ayers added that while working with recycled wood favors people living in suburban or rural areas, urban dwellers are not eliminated. Scrap yards can usually be found, if not right in the city, at least on the perimeter. In addition, with the large amount of renovating being done on inner city homes, old wood is being ripped out and thrown aside, making a good supply source for recycled wood in the city.

THE ART OF TINKERING

Especially important to this concept of "recycling by adapting" is the venerable art of tinkering. It's an approach long practiced by farmers who fabricate special tools in their own workshops—a kind of prototyping before anything quite like it is on the market. Tinkering has become a key factor in the development of appropriate technology, and since low costs are critical, old materials are always being adapted for new uses.

Some publications specialize in reporting such developments. One is the *Co-Evolution Quarterly* (Box 428, Sausalito, CA 94965—one-year subscription: $8). Another is *Alternative Sources of Energy* (Route 2, Milaca, MN 56353—one-year subscription: $10). The magazine reports regularly on such projects as building your own solar water heater, and reviews tomes like the *Solar Self-Help Book.* A consistent contributor is John McGeorge, who is described as a "tinkerer's tinkerer."

Rodale Press editor James McCullagh profiled McGeorge under the heading, "The Tinkering Man," and included these observations:

> Tucked in the tidy town of Norwalk, Connecticut, is a tinkerer, John McGeorge, who believes that if Americans are to control more of their lives, they will have to use their hands, as well as their heads.
>
> McGeorge is convinced that Americans will have to pull some of the electric plugs which tie them to a wasteful system. "The trouble with most people," remarked McGeorge, "is that they depend on others to run their lives. And to make matters worse, today's machinery and technology are so complicated that few of us can understand them. I think we have to rely more on appropriate technology, on machines and devices we can understand and fix. We have to rely more on muscle power."

More of a tinkerer than a philosopher, this Norwalk man practices what he preaches. He realizes that it is not good enough to talk about ways to improve life; we need alternatives. We need tools.

A look around his backyard reveals a solar greenhouse, an outside refrigerator box, a pedal-power unit which can wash clothes and possibly saw wood, chickens, an old car equipped to run on regular gas for long trips and kerosene for short ones, and a pile of heating wood scavenged from the neighborhood.

Reaching back into his childhood for an idea, McGeorge decided to build a modified version of the old window box. He took a wooden packing box about 16-by-17-by-26 inches and covered it with aluminum flashing. The door, constructed of ½-inch plywood, was also covered with aluminum. He placed the "box" on his back porch.

To stabilize the temperature during those cold New England winters, McGeorge tried a couple of things. One approach was to seal the box as tightly as convenient and use a thermostatically controlled lamp to warm the contents when the temperature gets below 35 degrees. The other system he used was to bring warm air in from the house by use of a fan and ducts. The system, which will draw about 250 watt-hours per day, is designed to operate between 35 and 50 degrees. Thus, it does not keep foods frozen or make ice, nor does it work during the warmer months of the year.

McGeorge set out to design a low-power washing machine. First he acquired a five-gallon plastic trash can for a couple of dollars. He then attached a sink plunger to a rubber cord, which in turn was attached to a fixed overhead object. He finally hooked up his washing machine to a bicycle.

No matter how gifted McGeorge is around the house, his low-technology point of view looks toward the community. He has scavenged enough wood from his neighborhood to keep his house warm for the winter. He gladly collects his neighbors' leaves for garden compost. He visits the local bakery and gets a large sack of scraps for his poultry (they seem to thrive on it).

CONSTRUCTING SOLAR-HEATED GADGETS

In the backwoods of Maine, Silas Weeks combines his tinkering with the sun, building a solar-heated shower and a food dryer from materials found around his 19th-century farmhouse. The solar-heated shower is made from an old metal drum, rubber tubing, and an old shower head. The metal drum, painted black to absorb and retain the heat, is situated above the showerhead on a small platform. Tubing runs down from the drum to the showerhead. A valve controls the water pressure. The barrel can be opened up to collect rainwater. During dry spells it is filled manually.

The food dryer is made from an old metal drum, painted black with about one-third of the barrel's side cut away. Shelves were made from old window screens to allow the hot air to circulate between layers.

Basketball courts under a highway: "We must recognize that as new spaces become more difficult to find, old spaces will have to be seen in a new light."

A solar greenhouse can be constructed by using recycled materials from the scrap yard. Glass panes are usually in abundance as they are hard to recycle, and wood boards for the backside are not difficult to obtain. Designs for solar greenhouses can be found in many do-it-yourself books. Again, urban dwellers are not excluded from building a solar greenhouse or a food dryer, as long as they have some southern exposure and a few feet of porch. Locate a scrap yard, a design book, *et voilà*! An urban garden.

OLD TIRES CAN HELP THE ENVIRONMENT

While old tires lying on the side of the road or in the middle of a river can be very unsightly, if tied together correctly they can serve an environmental purpose. Tires have been used for flood control. At the same time, fish can use them for protection when the water is high.

Also, old tires have been used for landslide control. They are placed along the sides of the slope. Eventually, as the earth slides down the hill it gets trapped in the tires, causing a terraced effect which helps prevent erosion. In addition, the tires are gradually covered as the terraces are formed.

Recycling Your Community

Making things from trash that "never was" is not limited to your own backyard or garden. On a larger scale, eyesores in the community such as a dump or an abandoned sewage-treatment plant, through use of the recycling eye and citizen effort, can be turned into a recreational playground or a botanical garden. James McCullagh, in a book entitled *Ways to Play*, made the following comment:

> Recycling often means rethinking, relooking at an eyesore and discovering a thing of beauty; it is the magician's trick: turning a sow's ear into a silk purse.

When applying this theory to play space, McCullagh continues, "Recycling for play means that we take a new and daring look at our environment and community, and recognize that as new spaces become more difficult to find, old spaces will have to be seen in a new light."

Several examples of municipalities across the country which have recycled instead of making parking lots are presented in *Ways to Play:*

Evanston, Illinois, transformed a city dumping mound into a ski slope, creating a multiple-use winter sports area. "It was once one end of the city dump. The hill was made of hunks of concrete, clay, dirt, and other inorganic garbage. That's how it got its name, 'Mt. Trashmore.'...The hill was sodded over, the slopes lined with clusters of evergreens, and sculpted into a picturesque 'Rocky.'"

The hill is used not only for skiing, but also for sledding and tobogganing. A snow-making machine was installed to extend the skiing season. Evanston is an example of a "community taking charge of its own recreation, of a community which gives the science of recycling an aesthetic dimension."

To the east of Evanston, in Miamisburg, Ohio, lies another community "recycle for play" effort. This town converted an abandoned sewage-treatment plant into a neighborhood park. Initially, residents complained about the odor of the plant, eventually causing it to cease operations. After that they complained that the unused plant was an eyesore in the neighborhood and served no purpose. Children, however, loved to play on the equipment, which was a safety hazard if unsupervised. Citizens and community leaders put two and two together and realized that with very little effort the sewage-treatment plant could be converted into a playground.

"Sludge beds are being converted into areas for basketball, volleyball, stick-hockey, and a regulation tennis court. The aero-clarifier will serve as a wading pool and a roller skating area. The digester will become an adventure playground for the younger boys and girls." As the recreational director of the park exclaimed, "The ugly duckling has hatched into a beautiful swan."

Elsewhere across the nation examples of recycling urban space abound. In Seattle, Washington, the Seattle Gas Works, once viewed as a "neo-Gothic nightmare of industrial blight which should be torn down," has also been converted into a park. "Now children, gleeful and whooping, romp, rollick, scoot, scamper, and climb through, over, and around wildly painted great chunks of machinery which once helped make the gas that lighted Seattle's streets."

Once the end of a city dump in Evanston, Illinois, this hill—made from hunks of concrete, clay, and inorganic garbage—is now used for skiing, sledding, and tobogganing.

Two other municipalities cited in *Ways to Play* were Eugene, Oregon, and an area in Los Angeles County, California. In Eugene, the city put in basketball courts under highway bridges where empty spaces are plentiful. In Los Angeles County an 87-acre hole filled with 3½ million tons of trash is now a unique botanical garden.

Across the country, 1,800 feet away from the Statue of Liberty, you can find yet one more example of recycling public space. In Jersey City, New Jersey, an old railyard is being converted into a park and a community cultural center. Michelle Galler explains in "From Old Rail Yard to New City Park" (*Smithsonian*, November 1978) how a Jersey City clothing retailer, Morris Pesin, took his family on a ferry to visit the Statue of Liberty. When they arrived, he saw "just a few hundred feet across the water, a decayed and dismal-looking urban waterfront—and realized to his dismay that it was a part of Jersey City." The abandoned railroad terminal of the Central Railroad of New Jersey with its "dilapidated railway cars, rusting tracks, and rotting docks—made a disgraceful backdrop for a very special national monument."

Morris Pesin took that ferry ride in 1958. From that time, Pesin made it his civic duty to transform that "disgrace" into a pleasant site/sight. He became a city councilman and "made the creation of 'Liberty Park' a priority, and badgered the state and federal governments for money to acquire land."

Thirty-five acres of Liberty Park were opened in 1976. Ultimately it will encompass 800 acres. "It will be almost as big as New York's Central Park, and will also realize a bold plan in urban landscape architecture. It will include a crescent-shaped, harbor-front promenade backed by trees and meadows, and a two-mile-long serpentine waterway. The huge and historic terminal building will be refurbished to provide sites for concerts, meetings, and a farmer's market. The Corps of Engineers is dismantling and hauling

Old railroad ties serve as excellent steps in a municipal garden.

away old docks and sunken ships so that marshlands can be restored."

One area of the park is being developed as a wildlife refuge. The terminal will also be used for cultural events. Liberty Park, once a railyard and almost grabbed up by commercial developers to build a Disneyland-like amusement park, stands as a final example of how a community can apply the "recycling eye" to trash that "never was."

Developing a Conference Site

In Montreal several years ago, over $1.5 billion was spent to develop the 1976 Olympic site for international athletic competition. In Vancouver, also in 1976, only a fraction of that amount was spent to transform an abandoned army airport into an international conference center known as Habitat. While the difference between the two events is immeasurable, the mentality, money, and resources that went into constructing the two sites are quite comparable.

Suffice it to say that the planning and construction of the Olympic site included very little consideration of conserving natural resources and space. The Habitat site, on the other hand, was totally planned around using logs from the lumber mill upstream which were washed up on the banks, and redesigning the interior of the airplane hangars for use as conference centers.

Because of the abundant and free lumber, construction at Habitat is based entirely on the use of wood. Outside amphitheaters were constructed, the seating built into the sides of the hills overlooking the wooden stage. Sidewalks were constructed from wooden planks and were protected from inclement weather by overhangs built from the "recycled wood." Included in the site was a homemade playground for the children of people attending a conference. A seesaw was constructed out of an old wire spool and two wooden planks. Old tractor tires served as a jungle gym.

Inside the hangars the walls were paneled, making the conference center just as attractive as the inside of the Olympic swimming pool building. Wooden sculptures as well as wooden furniture are used in the interior design.

The difference between the Montreal Olympic site and the Habitat Conference Center stands as an excellent example of what can be done if recycling of waste is included in the planning. Of course, the facilities needed for the Olympic competition cannot be compared to what is needed at a conference center, but the stark contrast between the levels of environmental consciousness is easily measurable.

Recycling became the working concept for the creation of Habitat in Vancouver in 1976. This seesaw made from old cable wire spools was typical.

Recycling Your Lifestyle

Day in and day out, we are continuously creating trash that does not have to be. With a little conscious effort, like taking advantage of car pools or conserving on electricity use, we can stop making excess trash by not generating excess waste. In older times personal conservation efforts were better known as "being thrifty"; now, in modern times, they are known as "voluntary simplicity."

Mark Satin, in an article for *New Age* magazine (October 1978), offers 80 ways to "lead a simpler life...living in a way that is outwardly simple and inwardly rich. This way of life embraces frugality of consumption, a strong sense of environmental urgency, a desire to return to living and working environments which are of a more human scale, and an intention to realize our higher human potential—both psychological and spiritual—in community with others."

In a section on clothing, Satin suggests such recycling ideas as developing a perspective on your clothes-buying habits, evaluating your true needs, swapping clothing, buying used clothing, and of course, making your own clothing, possibly from used garments. Some suggestions on how to conserve in furnishing your home include using homemade decorations, eliminating unnecessary appliances, sharing tools and appliances with others, reusing furniture, and in general employing energy-saving techniques through insulation or by installing solar heating and cooling systems.

Other lifestyle conservation ideas are to avoid disposable paper products, make compost, recycle papers and metals, avoid unnecessary travel and car use, use public transportation when possible, use simple personal products, educate yourself about your body, rediscover your community and its cultural events and sporting activities, give creative gifts, enjoy participatory and inexpensive sports, and watch your weight!

Satin's suggestions are uncomplicated and simple to implement.

The trick to it all is reorienting your mentality, thinking conservation and reuse instead of "I can always get more." Making things from "trash that never was" is not just confined to giving your newspaper to the Boy Scout drive or taking your bottles to the recycling center. At home, it means being creative in reusing things and being conservative in energy and water use. At the community level, it means turning abandoned buildings or railroad yards into community entertainment centers and parks. Waste recycling is not confined to resource-recovery machines. It requires individual and community cooperation and participation.

Children in Brookhaven, Long Island, New York, demonstrate how city leaves can be converted into valuable soil-building material via composting.

The Smallest and Best Recycling Center—Your Own Compost Heap*

For millions of home gardeners in the United States, the best recycling takes place right in the backyard. Instead of placing vegetable and fruit peelings from the kitchen in a garbage pail for removal by the collectors, these persons place the wastes in a *compost heap*.

When they mow grass or rake leaves, they don't gather them up and stuff them into plastic bags. Instead, those materials provide great stuff for the compost.

Composting in your own backyard is a public virtue that is being practiced in private. Such recycling has been going on for a long time—there are even references to compost in the Bible. The end product accomplishes two important functions:

1. It helps grow more abundant crops.
2. It uses wastes safely, simply and effectively.

*The information on home composting in this chapter was prepared by Maurice Franz.

Here in America, composting was practiced even before 1776. And the colonists worked with what was available and abundant. In New England, they composted with fish—mostly cod. But down south in the Land of Cotton, they worked with cotton burrs.

Room can always be made for a compost pile or bin, which logically should be to one side of the garden and as close as possible to the driveway to speed and ease the handling of materials.

Once you start a composting program, you will find a great abundance of materials available—all wastes—free and for the taking. And in some cases, notably leaves and wood chips, your local street and road department may be happy to deliver by the load.

Composting involves mixing and combining nitrogenous and carbonaceous materials with air, soil, and moisture. When in the proper proportion, with a carbon/nitrogen ratio between 25 and 30 parts carbon to 1 part nitrogen, the pile will heat up, thanks to the bacteria which are ever-present.

The gardening homesteader should have little or at most moderate difficulty in obtaining a sufficient and steady supply of these materials—again, all "wastes." Here they are: leaves, wood chips, sawdust, city sludge, and animal manures from nearby pony farms, country dairies, and poultry farms. In these last instances, the proprietors have always been happy to have you take away a load of their overabundance.

The above are compostable materials that are supplied *away from* your place. But your home is not without its own resources. Grass clippings are an ideal substance with a C/N ratio of 20. Add to them the crop residues and the weeds from your garden, all of which should be heaped up (preferably within an enclosure for neatness) as soon as they are gathered.

Use Your Family Garbage

But the biggest single source of compost that your place

provides in never-failing abundance is the family garbage. These food leavings, a sure source of garden fertility, can also be a communitywide problem when they are improperly handled.

Garbage can no longer be ignored; it is not a public or private disgrace to be hauled away in silence from the back alley and then dumped on the environment in huge, undigested hunks of filth and glut.

Because all of us create garbage every day that we live and breathe, if you have a garden in your backyard, put your garbage to work in the compost pile. Here's how it's done.

Quite properly, garbage "belongs" in your compost pile because it contributes the needed nitrogen and bacteria which help the piles ignite or heat up. Don't be afraid to experiment when you compost with garbage. Do things your way, according to the rhythms and ways you run your place.

You can empty your family garbage right on the compost heap, and then cover it with soil and green residues, preferably chopped up. You can also mix the contents in your garbage pail with sawdust or wood chips, layering the mix into your compost heap. This practice places the carbonaceous material right next to the nitrogenous, where it is needed.

If you have a shredder, run the mixture through, depositing the aggregate on a thick layer of newspapers and then shoveling it onto the heap.

But however you handle it or combine it, be sure to recycle your garbage in the family compost pile. This simple operation not only means a more productive food garden and more lovely flowers in your beds and borders, it also reduces the workload of your local sanitation department—which perhaps can lead to lower taxes.

In building a compost pile, biochemist Raymond Poincelot, who teaches at the University of Connecticut, attains a balanced carbon/nitrogen ratio by making eight-inch layers of leaves, hay, sawdust, or wood chips and four-inch layers of animal manures, garbage, or blood meal. He favors the "Berkeley method" which can produce compost in two weeks, a process developed at the University of California. However, he notes, "it requires several turnings on a fairly rigid schedule." His operation is as follows:

A mixture of wastes in a ratio of two or three parts carbonaceous materials to one part nitrogenous materials is used, although the mixture should not contain more than 10 percent paper. A typical mixture consists of leaves, grass clippings, and dry manure; the leaves can be stored from the fall, grass clippings are readily available during the growing season, and dry manure can be purchased. [*Ed. Note:* Manure can be free for the hauling, but you have to develop your sources of supply.]

The rapidity of the Berkeley method requires that these mixed materials be shredded with a mechanical shredder or by making several passes with a rotary mower over small piles. The material is composted into heaps five feet high, by eight feet by four, which are kept moist during the next two weeks.

By the second or third day, the pile usually heats up. If not, the carbon/nitrogen ratio is probably too high for decomposition. It can be lowered by mixing a high-nitrogen source such as blood meal into the pile. [*Ed. Note:* Try adding more animal manure such as poultry droppings or garbage; blood meal is expensive.] The heap should be turned with a spading or turning fork on the fourth day so that it is thoroughly mixed. The turning or aeration is repeated on the seventh and tenth day, at which time the pile normally begins to cool off.

At the end of 14 days, the compost is generally ready for use. The starting materials will be somewhat recognizable, but should appear coarse, crumbly, and dark brown in appearance. If finer humus is desired, it may be sifted or allowed to decay further.

The big advantage of the above method lies in its speed. Composting can be carried out in the spring, summer, or fall, and large quantities of compost can be produced. But it does "require more labor on a fairly fixed schedule."

Recycling leaves is a great autumn exercise. It is extremely easy to shred large amounts of leaves with a rotary mower. Work with a sturdy wall—the side of the garage is fine. Pile the leaves in

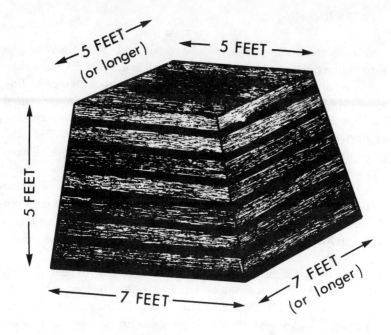

 8 inches of carbonaceous wastes

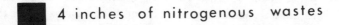 4 inches of nitrogenous wastes

Diagrammatic illustration of a well-made backyard compost pile shows repetition of layers.

(courtesy Raymond Poincelot)

windrows, and run the mower through and over them so the shredded aggregate bounces off the wall when it flies out of the chute of the mower and is conveniently piled. The rather fine aggregate that results can then be mixed with garbage or animal manure, kept moist, and turned every three days. Leaves are fine compostable material because of their high mineral content—the trees' deep-delving roots bring up valuable soil minerals which have leached down beyond the reach of other plant roots.

Don't be discouraged if you run into disappointments or difficulties. Occasionally—it can be often—a compost pile does not decompose when it should. Composting is the result of microbiological activities; it requires warmth, moisture, oxygen, and a 25 or 30-to-1 mixture of carbon and nitrogen.

One frequent difficulty is the failure of the pile to heat up. This can be the result of too much or not enough moisture, which can lower or even stop the heat-generating microbiological activity. This condition is easily corrected by drying out an overwet heap or by wetting a dry one.

Other conditions can adversely affect the microbiological activity necessary to reach the higher temperatures (from about 130 to 150 degrees Fahrenheit). These include insufficient nitrogen sources, which can be corrected by adding such nitrogenous materials as animal manures, grass clippings, and garbage. Or the pile can be too small, which can be corrected by enlarging it to provide more insulation. When the temperature outside the pile is too low, you can insulate the pile with burlap, soil, or leaves. Or you can wait for the weather to warm up.

Still another problem you may run into is the odor of ammonia or hydrogen sulfide. The first is caused by the carbon/nitrogen ratio's being too low. You can correct this by adding such carbonaceous materials as hay, sawdust, or leaves. The second is the result of anaerobic (without air) decay and can be corrected by turning the pile to get air back into it.

One way to avoid the problems and difficulties cited above is to control your C/N ratio. Keeping in mind that the ideal carbon/nitrogen ratio is between 25 and 30 to 1, here is a list of some materials that you can work with, and their carbon/nitrogen ratios:

Chicken droppings	7
Chicken litter	10
Cattle droppings	12
Food wastes	15
Weeds	19
Grass clippings	20
Fruit wastes	35
Leaves	60
Straw	100
Paper	170
Sawdust	450

These figures stand for parts of carbon to one part of nitrogen. Thus, chicken droppings are composed of seven parts of carbon to one of nitrogen. At the other end of the scale, sawdust is 450 parts of carbon to one of nitrogen.

If you want to make up some mixtures with a safe C/N ratio between 25 to 30 carbon to 1 part nitrogen, here are some workable combinations:

12 parts lawn clippings, 1 part sawdust	C/N 29
2 lawn clippings, 3 weeds, 1 leaves	C/N 28
2 leaves, 1 sawdust, 2½ cattle droppings	C/N 26
2 fruit wastes, 1½ lawn clippings	C/N 29
4 weeds, 3 paper, 1 chicken litter	C/N 27

Now, as the car manufacturers say in their ads, these are average figures. Actual contents of the different materials will vary according to the source and region. But on the whole, these are good, practical working proportions involving the materials you will be using.

Decomposer Organisms

Millions of tiny organisms dwell in and around organic litter, mainly *decomposer* organisms and their associates. Their effect is to transform plant and animal debris into soil humus.

Professor Daniel L. Dindal, a soil ecologist at SUNY College of Environmental Science and Forestry in Syracuse, New York, has illustrated the food web pattern of a compost pile (see the illustration).

Microorganisms such as bacteria, actinomycetes, and fungi are of major importance in the food web as the initial decomposers; also, many other organisms, like protozoa and roundworms, feed directly on them. Specific groupings or communities of protozoa develop at a site depending on the nature of the organic debris and the bacteria and fungi present. For example, a coprophilic ("fecal-loving") protozoan community predominates in manure or fecal deposits, while polysaprobic ("very rotten") protozoan communities are usually common in anaerobic decomposition sites. In terms of numbers of individuals, nematodes (roundworms) are frequently one of the most abundant invertebrates in decomposing organic matter. Nematodes control bacterial populations by harvesting them while processing the solid-waste material. Mold mites are white, transparent to translucent, soft-bodied creatures that feed on yeasts and other fungi related to fermenting conditions. Their presence can also be indicative of localized anaerobic conditions. Beetle mites (hard-boiled oribatid mites) and springtails (primitive insects) also feed on molds, but usually in organic waste under drier, more aerobic circumstances.

Some of the first interesting creatures to become established in waste deposits are the true decomposer organisms that feed and digest directly the items of wasted debris (1° or first-level consumers). Other creatures, known as second-level consumers (2°), feed on the initial decomposers. Still other organisms (3° or third-

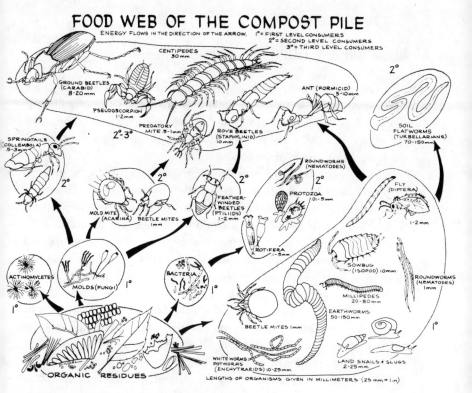

FOOD WEB OF THE COMPOST PILE

ENERGY FLOWS IN THE DIRECTION OF THE ARROW.   1°= FIRST LEVEL CONSUMERS
2°= SECOND LEVEL CONSUMERS
3°= THIRD LEVEL CONSUMERS

CENTIPEDES
30 mm

GROUND BEETLES
(CARABID)
8-20 mm

PSEUDOSCORPION
1-2 mm

ANT (FORMICID)
5-10 mm

2°

SOIL
FLATWORMS
(TURBELLARIANS)
70-150 mm

PREDATORY
MITE .5-1 mm

2°-3°

ROVE BEETLES
(STAPHYLINID)
10 mm

SPRINGTAILS
(COLLEMBOLA)
.5-3 mm

2°

ROUNDWORMS
(NEMATODES)

2°

FLY
(DIPTERA)

1-2 mm

PROTOZOA
.01-.5 mm

2°

FEATHER-
WINGED
BEETLES
(PTILIIDS)
1-2 mm

MOLD MITE
(ACARINA)

BEETLE MITES
1 mm

ROTIFERA
1-5 mm

SOWBUG
(ISOPOD) 10 mm

ROUNDWORMS
(NEMATODES)
1 mm

ACTINOMYCETES

1°

MOLDS (FUNGI)   1°

BACTERIA

1°

MILLIPEDES
20-80 mm

EARTHWORMS
50-150 mm

BEETLE MITES 1 mm

LAND SNAILS & SLUGS
2-25 mm

1°

ORGANIC   RESIDUES

WHITE WORMS
POTWORMS
(ENCHYTRAEIDS) 10-25 mm

LENGTHS OF ORGANISMS GIVEN IN MILLIMETERS (25 mm = 1 in)

This illustration, by Prof. Daniel Dindal, reveals the
range of nonhuman workers in the composting
process.

level consumers) prey on the second group and upon each other.
Such a feeding–predator–prey regime helps control and maintain
the decomposer community in the most stable, efficient condition.
As all these organisms ingest and digest, bound energy and nutrients
from organic materials are released, divided, and spread throughout
all the creatures and ultimately into the immediate environment.
This intricate scheme of energy and nutrient transfer among
organisms is known as a food web.

Locating and Building the Piles

Try to locate the pile in a sunny part of the yard with good air movement, as close to the driveway as possible. The sun will help the pile heat up while a moderate breeze encourages aeration. And the closer you are to the driveway, the less lugging you will have to do from your truck or station wagon.

Many experts recommend getting your pile up off the ground eight to ten inches, to encourage aeration by convection. This, plus the sunlight, means that your pile will have a tendency to dry out, so you will have to be extra-conscientious in keeping it moist.

You can make a good, practical compost bin in a couple of hours using cement building blocks, preferably "seconds" that are imperfect. But don't follow our recommendation blindly. If you have a good supply of old lumber around, be sure to use that.

Whatever you use, if you make a double bin with a partition in the center, you will be able to run two piles, one "building" and the other ready for use. For extra ventilation and economy, leave about three inches of space between the blocks, stacking them alternately in successive rows. Later, when the three-foot-high double bin is completed, thrust lengths of old pipes through the openings—they form a firm base for your piles.

Start the pile with branches or brushwood—pine or spruce boughs are excellent. Over this, add a layer of straw, and then manure or garbage. We favor adding a layer of good garden soil because of its large bacterial colony. Moisten (but do not drench) the layers with a fine spray from the garden hose as you add them. Be sure, as you continue, to alternate the nitrogenous and carbonaceous layers, making the carbonaceous layers twice as deep or thick as the nitrogenous.

So your pile should build up—straw followed by manure, followed by leaves, followed by garbage, followed by sawdust, followed by grass clippings (if available). Some gardeners top off the pile with a layer of soil, making a depression or "dish" in the center to catch and hold rainwater. Such a pile, adequately moistened, should start to heat up within three days.

Remember that the moisture content of a compost heap is very important. If it drops below 40 percent, the organic matter will not decompose rapidly. But if it runs over 60 percent moisture, not enough air can get into the heap. It is best to aim at 50 to 55 percent moisture, about the moisture content of a dampened sponge when it feels damp but not soggy.

Proper ventilation is no less important. Researchers stationed at Phoenix, Arizona, have found that a ton of rapidly decomposing compost—that's a pile about four feet high by four feet square—uses up 18,000 to 20,000 cubic feet of air daily. Most significant, they decided that turning the pile doesn't always get the job done. But convection, or "forced air" composting when the pile is up off the ground, stimulates uniform decomposition of the entire pile. This can be good news because it means you don't have to wrestle with a ton of compost every three days.

To recap, put your pile up off the ground in a sunny, breezy place, keep it moist but not soaking, and try to build it as close to the driveway as possible.

Should You Grind or Shred?

Many experienced composters feel that shredding is essential to rapid, successful composting. This does not necessarily mean that you have to buy one of the mobile, durable machines that have been designed particularly to reduce your compostables to an easily handled aggregate. You can get a great deal of chopping and shredding done with your rotary mower.

Chopping material into small bits increases their total surface, which makes it easier for the bacteria to work on them. The finer the particles, the faster they will be consumed. After some experimenting, you will work out a technique for mixing your materials as you grind them.

A good method for handling sludge and/or the family garbage is to mix them with wood chips or sawdust as you feed them into the shredder. If you are working with a mower, run it over heaps of loosely piled weeds or rows of leaves. Again, make use of a sturdy wall or fence to pile up the aggregate as it flies out the mower's chute.

The main advantage of owning and operating a shredder is that it helps to perfect your composting techniques. Today's shredder is sturdy and dependable, designed to take hard knocks and do a job. Well balanced, with a pair of rugged wheels, it is highly mobile and can be brought to the work. You will find how important this can be when a truckload of leaves, sludge, or wood chips is dumped next to your driveway. And once you build up your composting technique, there's always something that requires shredding and mixing, in and out of season. Whether you compost with the aid of a shredder or rotary mower, you'll find that it speeds and eases the tasks of chopping, shredding, grinding, and mixing the composting ingredients.

Getting the Materials

Believe it or not, this is one of the most enjoyable chores involved in composting. It gets you out into the country to talk with a lot of different people you otherwise would not meet. And in addition, you are performing a highly social function, the conversion of organic wastes into a substance that will be absorbed into the environment without harm or injury.

If you need sawdust, save the chore for a Saturday morning or afternoon, about an hour before the noon or late closing. That's the time to arrive at the back entrance of your local building-supply dealer or sawmill. They're always glad to have you haul away sawdust, emptying their bins or containers.

Or if you're looking for ground-up corncobs, or husks or hulls, take time out to visit your local feed mill. They ordinarily have a glut of these materials, and are only too happy to have you fill the burlap sacks, bushel baskets, or cardboard containers you brought along for this purpose.

Digested sewage sludge from your community wastewater-treatment plant is another material that should be in your composting piles (and also around your trees, shrubs, and ornamentals as a soil conditioner). Pay your plant a visit; the sludge may even be delivered free, right to your place, if you can handle a truckload. Be sure to ask about the quality of the sludge (i.e., heavy-metal content) and suggested application procedures.

The same applies to your community's leaves. You might even get them delivered free to your house—if you can take a truckload. Check with city hall. In many communities, composted leaves are offered—sometimes for a nominal charge, sometimes free. Composted leaves are ideal for the garden, and can be used in the compost pile or as a mulch in the garden row.

And manure! Together with your garbage, this is the spark that ignites your compost pile. You may have to go further and work harder to obtain a steady and sufficient supply, but you will find that the result more than justifies the effort.

Wood chips are still another commonly available material. Keep your eye open for the power company or public maintenance crews when they are out trimming the growths along your nearby county roads and shredding them on the spot with a chipping machine. Tell the crew captain you live nearby; he'll often be glad to drop a load of chips off at your place instead of driving all the way back to the community dump. Recommended practice is the same as for compost piles—keep two piles of wood chips, one for immediate use while the other is maturing.

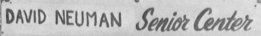

DAVID NEUMAN *Senior Center*
Demonstration Garden

URBAN GARDENING
PROGRAM

Cooperative Extension Service
The Pennsylvania State University

Urban areas as well as rural ones can benefit from compost. These views of a Philadelphia Urban Gardening Program show how city-created wastes (from garbage
and sludge to leaves) can turn barren lots into food-producing plots.

(courtesy Cooperative Extension Service, Pennsylvania State University and the U.S. Department of Agriculture)

Compost Bins

While there have been many variations in design and materials, the ideal compost bin lets light and air get at the pile while it discourages the neighborhood cats, dogs, and other four-legged predators. A well-constructed compost bin also adds to the general neatness of the garden and yard—it keeps things from blowing all over the place.

But work with what you've got, what you can get cheap or free in your area, and don't be bound by convention. Use wood, concrete blocks, metal wire fencing, piping—anything that's "surplus" in your community. That's practicing recycling, too. Here are some "classic" bins that gardeners have been using to make compost for more than half a century.

The Wood and Wire Bin is made of half-inch chicken-wire mesh framed by two-inch-square scrap lumber. It consists of two *L*-shaped sections, held together with screen-door hooks. Each of the four sides is three feet square, which makes for a three-by-three structure, three feet high.

Gardeners who work with this lightweight, easily handled unit report that the pile should be turned every three or four days, damping down each layer—leaves, grass, garbage, manure—as it is turned. They advise that the well-ventilated cage—the air gets at it from all sides—encourages complete bacterial action.

Turning is easy. Unhook two opposite sides, making two *L*-shaped sections, and reassemble them next to the square-shaped heap which stands neatly square. Then, using a turning fork, peel off the layers, tossing them into the empty cage. As noted, keep the hose handy to wet down the heap while transferring the materials.

The Wooden New Zealand Box is rated a "classic" which was originally designed by the Auckland Humic Club to admit "as much air as possible" from all sides. Many variations exist, so don't hesitate to make yours fit the needs and contours of your garden and yard.

One design calls for one-by-two wood slats nailed securely to two-by-two framing at half- to three-quarter-inch intervals. It's a good idea, if possible, to locate the bin (two bins are better than one) in a sunny corner of the back fence which would serve as two sides of the unit. Some gardeners have separated the twin bins with sliding partitions which they lift out when turning the pile.

We also recommend making a pair of wooden bases to get the pile up 10 inches off the ground. Make them three or four feet

Well-constructed compost bins maintain neatness in the garden, allow easy access for turning materials.

square—whichever is convenient—using one-by-six lumber, with two-by-two legs at the corners and also in the center of each side. That's eight legs—four at the corners and four in the middles for each base. Cover the top with two sections (for extra strength) of half-inch heavy-duty wire netting, using extra-rugged staples to secure them to the frame. Made conscientiously, and topped off with a weathering dressing of linseed oil, these compost-pile bases should give you years of good service.

Steel Drum Composters have been made by the gardener who

By composting wastes, you begin to achieve a self-sufficiency in which nothing is wasted and the community's social load is lightened.

wants to compost in a congested suburban neighborhood. The problem is not to offend your neighbors while achieving a satisfactory compost. The bottom of the steel drum is perforated with holes (one-half to one inch), and then set on eight-inch cement blocks, which gets them up into the air.

Revolving Drum Composters have been built by several ambitious gardeners who appreciate the importance of getting air into the pile. An extra, built-in advantage to this method is that it mixes the various ingredients while ventilating them. But while the revolving drum technique eliminates turning, it also calls for extra damping down because of the abundant ventilation of the pile. Some commercial models are now on the market.

Whatever bin you make and use, follow your own needs and garden methods. If you work with wood, "weather" it by applying a coat of linseed oil to prevent rot. Give the coated lumber about three days to absorb the oil and dry out before starting composting operations.

As we have seen, running a compost pile involves many skills. You have to be handy with tools, ready to meet people and talk around, and willing to haul and tote. In addition, it helps to be creative and imaginative, quick to see an opportunity to do a thing a new way, and happy to take a chance on it.

Composting is a function which makes full use of your home's resources, and further enhances them through recycling. Using—not wasting—your crop residues, your grass clippings, your weeds is just plain common sense in these times of rising inflation. By composting them with your family garbage, you are beginning to achieve a self-sufficiency in which nothing is wasted and the community's social load is lightened.

In addition, you raise better, more nutritious and abundant crops and lovelier, more colorful flowers.

By all means—make compost!

Recycling Waste on the Home Woodlot

Dr. Geoffrey Stanford, director of the Greenhills Environmental Center in Cedar Hill, Texas, presented an intriguing idea for recycling—akin to the composting concept—at the 1978 meeting of the American Society of Agricultural Engineers. Briefly, Dr. Stanford proposed that any family living on about a half acre should consider using its "domestic manures" to increase yield from a home woodlot, and thereby recycle waste into energy. Dr. Stanford explains that in Europe, where wood for fuel is scarce, people have long recognized that new sprouts grow from the stumps after the trees have been felled. The regrowth is often stronger from the younger trees than from the older, and this management cycle can be repeated almost indefinitely. This form of husbandry, known as coppicing, deliberately encourages new sprouts to grow from the stumps of felled trees. Eventually, this wood can serve as firewood. "A well-run coppice," says Dr. Stanford, "can be expected to yield eight to ten tons of dry wood per hectare [about 2½ acres] per year from the third cycle onward."

Dr. Stanford then goes on to say that a family of five uses in waste about 2,000 liters (about 525 gallons) of clean water each day. This waste water contains a variety of substances, many of which are good plant nutrients:

> When the family wastewaters are used to irrigate their coppice, this nutrient-enriched water percolates through the leaf litter, the topsoil, and the subsoil, and eventually leaves the forest as surface streams and as aquifer recharge, fresh, clean, and pure, fit for drinking again.

He also foresees that a coppice energy plantation is a "singularly suitable place in which to deposit refuse. . . . a canopy cover quickly forms, and the refuse is soon hidden from sight under the spreading leaves; biodegradation proceeds, encouraged by the irrigation with the nitrogen-rich sewage waters, which further increases the yield above dryland productivity levels....So, all the available information suggests that a family will benefit many times over by using their coppice woodlot as the ultimate sink for their wastes. They will get more fuel wood; they will recycle their waste waters on their own land and cleanse them there for reuse; they will retain the nutrients that they have imported; and they will have eliminated the cost, both in dollars and energy, of disposal."

Closing the Cycle with a Greenhouse

Another concept that relates to Dr. Stanford's is one developed by Abby Rockefeller and Carl Lindstrom, specifically for use by owners of compost toilets. The idea involves the application of "graywater" in the greenhouse. Writes Ms. Rockefeller:

> When toilet and kitchen wastes are deposited in a compost converter and thus prevented from ever being mixed with the water, there are several favorable consequences to the wastewater —now graywater—leaving the house: (1) there is less of it—about 40 percent; (2) there are only small particles and fibers such as hair, lint, little bits of food washed down the drain, which can better be removed by a roughing filter than by a septic tank; (3). the character of the organic and nutrient content is such that it has a much more rapid breakdown than total sewage or "blackwater."
>
> We will describe here how a greenhouse can neatly close the cycle of organic waste conversion/water purification/food production. Our description is based on an arrangement consisting of a Clivus Multrum, a Lindstrom roughing filter, and a lean-to greenhouse. It has been in operation for a little over one year in Cambridge, Massachusetts. The critical aspects are deep soil boxes in the greenhouse, an irrigation/purification interaction between the graywater and soil boxes, and a rock storage under the greenhouse floor for heating and cooling.
>
> All the washwater passes through a stone roughing filter which serves the function of preventing the particles in the graywater

from plugging up the small holes in the leach lines, which they would otherwise rapidly do. From the roughing filter, the effluent is automatically pumped into the greenhouse soil boxes by way of 1½" PVC pipes with ¼" holes every foot on the underside. These leach pipes lie 2"–3" under the soil surface. The soil boxes are 4' deep and 2' wide. There is altogether 54 sq.ft. of surface growing area. The soil mix consists of one-half homemade leafmold (produced in the backyard from neighborhood leaves and with the nutrients and warmth in the graywater before there was a greenhouse), and one-half commercial topsoil. This mixture is consistent to the bottom where there is a 2" layer of crushed rocks for good drainage, with a ¼" mesh screen on top and 1" of ½" stones. The soil boxes have drains at the low end of a slightly sloping bottom so that the water which is not taken up by plants and not absorbed in the soil can pass out.

The effect of a greenhouse used in this way should be the creation of a symbiotic relationship between the "interests" of the water (purification) and the "interests" of the growing plants (irrigation and nutrification).

Cutting Out Waste:
De Facto Recycling
Via Purchasing Power

In the last few years a variety of products has entered the marketplace that directly or indirectly benefit recycling. Some provide a way to use recyclable materials, adding an economic underpinning for reclaimed materials. Other products conserve energy and materials by reducing the amount of resources we consume for the services we seek.

This form of recycling can be accomplished by you as a consumer—as a customer and an important segment of the marketplace. Just think how great it will be when Coca-Cola or Schaeffer Brewery or Owens-Illinois says "We're using and making returnable bottles because the American consumer demands them." That day is coming, especially as more of us *recycle-ize* our purchasing standards.

A few simple ways come to mind quickly.

Buy products with recycled paper fibers, and always check the percentage of the recycled portion. More than half the garbage

Recycling symbol used by the American Paper Institute.

generated in our homes and offices and factories consists of paper. A common problem for all recyclers is fluctuating prices for reclaimed paper. The problem would be alleviated greatly if a strong consumer demand for paper products made from recycled fibers developed.

When you buy paper products of any kind, read the label carefully for a statement like "Made from Recycled Fibers." A few years back, the industry adopted a symbol denoting that fact, and you may find it on many items.

Bergstrom Papers of Neenah, Wisconsin, has been a leader in recycling wastepaper for years—it has never owned forests. (For every ton of reprocessed newsprint, the equivalent of 17 trees are saved—not to mention that disposing of a ton of papers can cost us about $50 in taxes.) Bergstrom's advertisements proudly and poetically state: "We make paper out of paper. We wash yesterday's history out of it. The ink. We beat out yesterday's clay. And resins. And fillers. And binders. A thread remains: A clean, pure fiber born long ago in a green forest." Bergstrom president Hugh R. Moore writes that his company has been recycling wastepapers to provide fiber "since shortly after the turn of the century. The major portion by far, finds its way into the book publishing field."

Bergstrom Paper Company is understandably proud of its role in our world of paper, stressing how it makes fine book stock from wastepaper. "America's cities are Bergstrom's forests....From the trees of steel and glass, we harvest shorter, flatter, smoother paper fibers that are a generation away from the damp, green forests of their birth. Combined with lesser quantities of long-fiber pulp, it results in a sheet of printing paper which possesses a number of unusually desirable characteristics."

Bergstrom is a good example of how a company can turn everyday wastes into an asset—more than 160 tons of wastepaper are converted daily. Just as important, the company stresses the recycled aspect of its product in its advertising program. You as a consumer play a vital role when you consciously seek out products made from reclaimed materials.

Another example of recycling via conservation relates to household water consumption. For example, there have been all sorts of homemade gadgets designed to "Stop the Five-Gallon Flush." Some use bricks, some use old plastic jugs.

In the past few years, hardware stores and plumbing supply stores have begun to stock several water-conserving devices, so if you prefer to buy rather than make one, you will now have a choice available.

Several companies have been established to assist you in household conservation efforts. One such is Domestic Environmental Alternatives, of Hathaway Pines, California, a small firm formed to provide homeowners with ways to conserve water and energy, and to improve upon individual on-site sewage-disposal systems. "Periodically," explains DEA's Janet Skenfield, "we offer free seminars to the community on such subjects as water conservation, alternative sewage disposal, and solar energy." They also have a retail store and distribute plumbing products stressing alternative low-water and waterless units. Such units include low-flow shower-heads, low-flush toilets, compost toilets, and washwater irrigation systems.

David del Porto and his firm called ECOS, Inc., in Allston, Massachusetts, are another example of commercial efforts aimed at individuals who see the unity between recycling and conservation. ECOS, Inc., specializes in composting toilets. After several years of pioneering efforts to market and service such devices, del Porto delivered these observations at a University of Massachusetts conference in 1977:

> The consumer demands an alternative which offers similar convenience, aesthetic appeal, and reliability to conventional water flush systems. The homeowner with a sanitary problem needs an effective solution at a reasonable cost. . . . The costs (and abuses) of central collection and waste treatment are becoming so staggering that many small and medium-sized communities are cracking under the strain of federally funded projects. . . . Herein we discover a virtue of the dry composting (recycling) concept: It reduces water consumption. By reducing and hopefully eliminating the volumes of drinking water used to carry human excreta, individual, municipal, and federal expenditures will be vastly reduced. Imagine the effect of such conservation methods on sewer and waste-treatment plant construction costs.

The new on-site treatment systems are being studied, demonstrated, publicized, and increasingly installed. Thanks to effective research done at such places as the Farallones Institute and Integral

Large model.

Small container assembled.

INSTALLATION

The CAROUSEL consists of:
1. Outer container
2. Inner container
3. Cover
4. Connecting pipe, length 1m (3' 4")
5. Commode
6. Flange for vent
7. L-bend
8. Vent pipe (not supplied)
9. Ventilator and couplings
10. 6" dia. pipe with storm collar, 1.5m (5') long.
11. Roof flashing
12. Vent hood

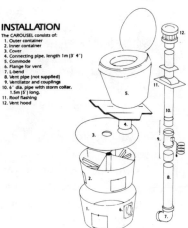

View into small container.

Reducing household water consumption is one example of recycling via conservation.
Devices such as this Carousel Compost Toilet, with a rotating chamber, offer a
commercial alternative to conventional water-flushed toilets.

Urban House in California, the Minimum Cost Housing Group at Montreal's McGill University, and elsewhere, solid information is being amassed for the benefit of consumers who want to recycle by using resources well in the first place. And the number of "brand names" is proliferating: Toa-Throne, Clivus Multrum, Humus Toilet, Biu-Let, Ecolet, and Bio-Loo.

You can use your individual and family purchasing power to buy products which aid recycling and resource conservation. And you can also use that power *not* to buy products which have a negative impact. Remember the "Trash Masher"? For years, I've saved a two-page advertisement from *Life* magazine which included these paragraphs:

> In the beginning, God created man. And promptly created trash. Now, in 1970, Whirlpool has finally created a civilized way to get rid of it: The Trash Masher Compactor. It fits under your kitchen counter, or plugs in anywhere. Whenever you have trash or garbage, simply toss it into the replaceable plastic-lined bag inside the drawer. You can even throw in bottles and cans. Then shut the drawer and turn it on....

The advertising copy for this "civilized" contraption then explained what a neat little package is created, how it's even sprayed with a deodorant, how your garbage man will love you. And the payoff was the seven-word conclusion: "The Trash Masher. Our contribution to civilization."

Obviously, Whirlpool was giving its machine an ecological coating when in fact, its unit complicated the later separation of wastes for recycling, and lulled the consumer into a false sense of environmental security.

Consumers need to learn how to use purchasing power to buy products which aid resource conservation, and *not* to buy products which simply add to the burden.

Plastic Food Packaging

At the household level, the best recycling strategy is often not to obtain the material in the first place. Consider packaging materials, which are now a $15-billion-a-year business. To be specific, consider the plastics that are replacing paper and bottles for many products. As you will see later, recycling centers are developing for household-sorted glass and metals, but plastics will drive the most ardent recycler up a wall. (More than 26 billion pounds of plastic were produced in the U.S. in 1977.)

The list of foods now packaged in plastics is rapidly increasing: orange juice, breakfast cereals, soda, and on and on. First we saw the demise of the milk bottle, and now we are witnessing the end of paper cartons. New ways have been found to package food at high speeds on machines that form and fill plastic, and the big push is underway to use the technology for packaging greater amounts of our food.

An effort to thwart the greater plasticizing of America is being led by a combination of environmentalists, health officials, and packagers who supply paper, cans, and bottles (not plastic, of course). Critics cite the fact that plastic is derived from petroleum, is not biodegradable, creates toxic smoke when burned; and that certain plastics like acrylonitrile can migrate from the package to the food, thereby creating a potential carcinogenic problem. Some government agencies are trying to regulate plastic packaging use. The Minnesota pollution-control agency banned the sale of milk in throwaway plastic containers, and the Oregon legislature outlawed plastic rings on six-packs. The federal Food and Drug Administration has proposed a ban on acrylonitrile, and bans on polyvinyl chloride (PVC) packaging have also been proposed.

It's getting more and more difficult to avoid plastic packaging, but the best way to solve the recycling challenge is to bring as little as possible into your home.

Water Conservation

Back to the positive use of your purchasing power, recyclers will be particularly aided by obtaining a copy of *Water Conservation and the Mist Experience,* published by the Minimum Cost Housing Group of McGill University (School of Architecture, 3480 University St., Montreal, Quebec H3A 2A7, Canada; price, $4). After citing critical shortages of water in many parts of the world and early research in designing nozzles and other devices which make a little water go a long way, the publication then lists many

This Cycle-Let system, developed by the Thetford Corp., treats wastes from five toilets and two urinals, then processes and recycles wastewater, thus conserving water.

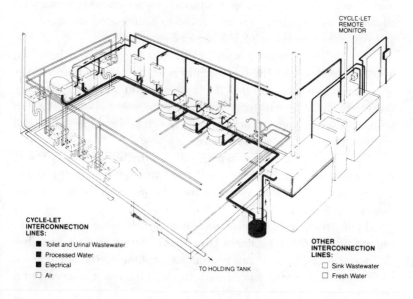

CYCLE-LET
REMOTE
MONITOR

CYCLE-LET
INTERCONNECTION
LINES:

■ Toilet and Urinal Wastewater
■ Processed Water
■ Electrical
□ Air

TO HOLDING TANK

OTHER
INTERCONNECTION
LINES:

□ Sink Wastewater
□ Fresh Water

commercial sources in a catalogue section. The authors—Alex Morse, Vikram Bhatt, and Witold Rybczynski—write:

> We feel that devices such as these deserve wider application. No longer is water conservation an issue that is restricted only to arid regions, though of course it is most serious there. Today, as water treatment and sewage treatment become increasingly expensive, the conservation of water has become increasingly important all over the world, whether in Arabian Gulf boom towns, squatter settlements in Southeast Asia, or in North America.

The catalogue section then lists the variety of water-conserving devices now on the market: pressure-reducing valves, flow restrictors, metering faucets, faucet aerators, showerheads, temperature selectors.

Illustrating how water conservation is synonymous with energy conservation—both are obviously part and parcel of recycling philosophy—in March 1978 the Long Island Lighting Company of New York sent water-flow restricters to its 800,000 residential customers as an energy-saving measure. Anticipated savings were $50 per year per household in water-heating costs.

The utility company estimated that a typical shower lasts five minutes, that each of the four members of an average family takes one shower per day, and that the device would cut water used per shower from 40 gallons to 16. The company spent about $20,000 to send customers the restrictors, which resemble dime-size metal washers and fit into showerheads.

By conserving water and recycling directly certain types of wastewater, you'll greatly reduce the 100-gallon-per-person-per-day average for Americans. Annually, that figures to 88,000 gallons per family.

In an article for *Organic Gardening and Farming* magazine, "In Pursuit of the Zero-Discharge Household," Steve Smyser describes the many ways to save and recycle water. One of the best-known techniques is to place an ordinary brick in the toilet reservoir of a flush toilet, thereby displacing about one quart of water. Two one-quart plastic bottles, filled with water and weighted with a small stone to keep them in place, will accomplish the same thing—holding back water contained in the tank.

Commercial gadgets to reduce volume and improve float assemblies come in a wide array now. Some wall off a section of the toilet reservoir; float assemblies can be adjusted to maintain a lower water level. Shallow-trap toilets are also available, using about 3½ gallons per flush as compared to the standard 5 or 6.

Water savings can also be effected by installing devices to limit the rate of flow from showerheads and faucets. Whereas normal flow from conventional showerheads ranges from 5 to 15 gallons per minute, flow-control devices cut this rate to 3½ gallons per minute with no sacrifice in cleaning or general acceptability.

A list of some water-conserving hardware and sources follows.

Water-Conserving Hardware

The following is a partial listing of manufacturers with water-conserving devices currently on the market.

Toilet-Tank Volume Reducers
Aqua-Miser
Energy Recovery Systems, Inc.
P.O. Box 233
Lincroft, NJ 07738

The Fluidmaster Flusher Fixer Kit
Fluidmaster, Inc.
P.O. Box 4264
1800 Via Burton
Anaheim, CA 92803

Little John North Shore Assoc.
Greenhurst, NY 14742

Save-It Watersaver
Ny-Del Corporation
Glendora, CA 91740

The Water Gate
JKW 5000 Ltd.
10610 Culver Blvd.
Culver City, CA 90230

Water Wizard
Box 184
Croydon, PA 19020

Dual-Flush Devices
Dual Flush System
Savway Co., Inc.
930 Clarkson Ave.
Brooklyn, NY 11203

Duo-Flush
Ramsey Associates
Box 2406
Colorado Springs, CO 80901

Flush-Gard
Utah Marine
459 South 7th St.
Brigham City, UT 84302

Shallow-Trap Toilets
Conserver Briggs Corp.
5200 Kennedy Blvd.
Tampa, FL 33602

Emblem Water Saving Closet
Eljer Plumbingware
Gateway Bldg. #3
Pittsburgh, PA 15219

Microphor
(2 qt. flush with comp. air)
Box 490
Willits, CA 95490

Miniaqua
Kohler Co.
Kohler, WI 53044

Radcliffe Water Miser
Crane Company
300 Park Avenue
New York, NY 10022

Water Saver Cadet
American Standard
40 W. 40th St.
New York, NY 10018

Water-Saving Fixtures
Anyflow Shower Head With
Autoflo Flow Control
Conservaflo
Speakman Company
Wilmington, DE 19899

Aquamizer
American Standard
40 W. 40th Street
New York, NY 10018

Crane Crestmont
Crane Company
300 Park Avenue
New York, NY 10022

Bubblestream Ecology Water
Sewer Kit
Wrightway Manufacturing Co.
Distributed by G & S
Supply Co.
5801 S. Halsted St.
Chicago, IL 60621

Delta Faucet Co.
Greensburg, IN 47240

Dole Automatic Volume
Shower Controls
Eaton Corporation
Controls Division
191 East North Ave.
Carol Stream, IL 60187

Econo-Flo
The Chicago Faucet Co.
2100 South Nuclear Drive
Des Plaines, IL 60018

Ecology Water Saver
Wrightway Mfg. Co.
371-377 E. 116th St.
Chicago, IL 60628

Eljer Plumbingware
Gateway Bldg. #3
Pittsburgh, PA 15219

The Flushmate
Water Control Products
N.A., Inc.
110 Owendale, Suite E
Troy, MI 48084

Merwin 321
Merwin Manufacturing
136 E. Fourth Street
Dunkirk, NY 14048

Miniuse Shower Assembly
(.5 gram with comp. air)
206 N. Main Street
Jackson, CA 95642

Moen Easy-Clean
377 Woodland Ave.
Elyria, OH 44035

Noland Company
Newport News, VA 23607

Nova Controlled-Flow
Shower Heads
Water Wizard, Inc.
P.O. Box 184
Croydon, PA 19020

Nova Tool Tech Corp.
10A Water Street
Lebanon, NH 03766

Ny-Del Shower Heads &
Flow Controls
Ny-Del Corporation
P.O. Box 155
740 E. Alosta Ave.
Glendora, CA 91740

Rada 872
Richard Fife, Inc.
140 Greenwood Ave.
Midland Park, NJ 07432

Speakman Auto-Flo
Speakman Company
Wilmington, DE 19899

Symmons Engineering Co.
Boston, MA 02109

Ultraflo
Real Gas & Electric Co.
Box A
Guerneville, CA 95446

Ultraflow Push Button
One-Line Plumbing
Ultraflow Corporation
P.O. Box 2294
Sandusky, OH 44870

Unatap
Richard Fife, Inc.
140 Greenwood Ave.
Midland Park, NJ 07432

Water Gate Shower Head,
Flow Control, and
Conservarator
JKW 5000 Ltd.
10610 Culver Blvd.
Culver City, CA 90230

Once the connection between recycling and energy conservation is made, then the individual begins to fathom the breadth and depth of issues and activities involved. Nothing mysterious or terribly complex is involved, although the interlocking facets of daily routines have been eloquently set forth by a number of individuals like René Dubos, Barry Commoner, Buckminster Fuller, Bernard Dixon, Margaret Mead, Lewis Mumford, and countless others.

What we do with what we buy—and what we don't do with what we don't buy—directly affects what natural resources are used well or poorly, and whether or not recycling can be achieved simply or only after great effort. The consumer who decides to make use of solar energy, wood stoves, bicycles, and other tools of appropriate technology is practicing recycling at its most fundamental stage.

6

Start Off with a Tough One—Sludge

In Boston, it's called *Metroloam*; in Los Angeles, *Nitrohumus*. Chicago uses the term *Nu-Earth*. And Philadelphia, naturally, goes for *Philorganic*, having learned a lesson from Milwaukee's *Milorganite*.

Big cities and small towns are making their gardeners, nurserymen, landscapers, and park superintendents happy by developing successful programs for turning organic wastes into an abundant organic soil conditioner and fertilizer.

The land is being rediscovered as a place where organic wastes can be used effectively and economically. The legislation to end ocean dumping of sludge, the commitment to achieve energy savings from waste recycling, the urgency to control hazardous pollutants, the politics of applying wastes to private and public lands—these and other critical forces all encourage us to learn more about recycling treated sludge and wastewater.

Every man, woman, and child in this country who has access to a flush toilet produces about 100 gallons of sewage daily. Some recycling is accomplished by using the wastewater and its nutrients

As wastewater is treated at city sewage plants, sludge is separated. It can wind up either as a major problem or as a major resource.

At Beltsville, Maryland, sludge is mixed with other materials such as wood chips, then composted in windrow piles for 21 days while air is drawn through the materials.

as irrigation for farmland. At most metropolitan sewage-treatment plants, wastewater is treated and solids—called sludge—are separated. The sludge is classified as raw, digested, or activated, depending on the process used and the stage of treatment.

Our nation is rich in sludge, but putting that richness to use presents tremendous challenges—to mayors, council members, and public works officials; to residents who live near the treatment plant or near where the sludge may be used on land; to public health officials and researchers who are concerned about safety.

Composting is increasingly being viewed as a treatment process that will solve most, if not all, of the problems associated with sludge recycling. Whether done on a small or large scale, composting is a method of waste management whereby the organic component of the solid-waste stream is biologically decomposed under controlled conditions to a state in which it can be handled, stored, and/or applied to the land without adversely affecting our health or environment.

Based on its own research, the U.S. Department of Agriculture concluded that adding compost to a light, sandy soil increases water-holding capacity, and makes a heavy soil friable and loose. A few years ago, the USDA issued a report, *Compost: From Waste to Resource*, which stated:

> New applications of an old principle—composting of sewage sludge—score an E for excellence in preliminary tests for efficiency, economy, environmental soundness, and esthetic quality. Composting once was considered out of the question as a solution for the pressing needs for better waste disposal methods. However, research is answering many questions about the practicality of composting, including two crucial points. Can this age-old principle be modified to operate successfully on an urban scale? Can composting be conducted during cold, wet weather typical of most American cities for several weeks or months of the year?

The U.S. Environmental Protection Agency, saying most cities around the country already have the principal equipment necessary to adopt a relatively inexpensive process, is supporting the project at Bangor, Maine. Bangor officials estimate they will save in excess of 50 percent of their current annual expenditures for loam and mulch materials, which will now be replaced by compost. In addition, they are avoiding the expense of disposing of the sludge by incineration or landfill.

A University of California biologist notes how composting saves energy and recycles needed nutrients: "Resources are conserved directly by returning to the land the nutrients contained in the wastes (both macro- and micro-nutrients), and indirectly in the form of the energy that would otherwise be consumed in the production of chemical fertilizers."

Composting is being studied and practiced all over the country. One process, known as the Beltsville Aerated Pile Method, since it was developed at the USDA Research Center in Beltsville, Maryland, is now used at Durham, New Hampshire; Camden, New Jersey; Windsor, Ontario; and at pilot projects in Florida, Massachusetts, and California. Major installations have been proposed for Westchester County, New York, and for Washington, D.C.

In the Beltsville, composting process, the sludge is mixed with a bulking agent such as wood chips and then composted in a stationary pile for 21 days while air is drawn through the mass. The costs are relatively low, and a variety of waste materials can be used as a bulking agent to keep the pile "loose"—shredded paper, paper pellets, leaves, peanut hulls, and automobile fluff (shredded foam rubber and fabric material recovered after metal removal).

For more than 50 years, windrow composting has been the method used to turn wastes generated at the Los Angeles, California, County Sanitation District into a popular organic fertilizer called Kellogg's Nitrohumus. The sludge is shaped into long piles, or windrows, about 4 feet high and 10 feet wide, and then regularly turned by machine to insure adequate amounts of oxygen and temperature rise. After periods ranging from 21 days in summer to 40 days in winter, the Kellogg Company hauls the mature compost to its facilities for screening, bagging, and distribution.

Clay Kellogg of Carson, California, is one of the most knowledgeable people in the country when it comes to marketing sludge. When his father started the Kellogg Supply Company in 1925, the sludge was sold and spread on farmland, mainly citrus, throughout the Orange County area. Today, his customers are retail nurseries, wholesale nursery growers, landscapers, golf courses, parks, etc. As Kellogg points out: "When I say sewage sludge, I mean a well-digested and composted sewage that no longer is a raw organic, but rather a humus product, without any unpleasant odor.... We call our product Nitrohumus.... All we need is a positive attitude and sewage sludge will be an important part of the future."

Repeatedly we have heard people say: "The problems with sewage sludge wouldn't be nearly as bad if it didn't have an ugly name like sludge." John Lear, former science editor of *Saturday Review*, commented a few years ago on the semantic inadequacy of the word *"sludge"*:

> Solution of the waste problem will have to begin on a semantic level. With typical disregard of the effects of technical jargon on the lay mind, sanitary engineers long ago dubbed the valuable resource that human waste represents as "sewage sludge." In response to mental attitudes shaped by the sometimes unrealistic perspective of modern urban society, many people must force themselves to think of sewage in any positive terms. And so is error compounded. For the so-called sludge is as different from raw sewage as broken eggs are from a home-baked cake.

But, by any name, the materials present a complex challenge to recyclers. That's why a well-planned, broad-based strategy of composting sludge is so critical. Some regions are now facing the challenge head-on. The Garden State of New Jersey, for example, planning for the 1981 federal ban on ocean dumping, is energetically developing a statewide sludge-composting project. Professor Mark Singley of the Rutgers Agricultural Engineering Complex belongs to a team of soil scientists, microbiologists, horticulturists, and sanitary engineers who are working with cities like Camden to put composting principles into widespread use.

The Camden sludge compost facility: (1) step van from Rutgers containing continuous temperature-recording instruments and other laboratory facilities; (2) aerated extended pile; (3) curing pile; (4) unassembled screening unit; (5) nearby residential houses; (6) Rutgers research area; (7) stockpiled wood chips; (8) blower assembly; (9) scrubber pile; (10) aeration headers with underground pipe connections.

An Example in New Jersey

Because New Jersey is so densely populated—close to 1,000 people per square mile—and because about 85 percent of its population is served by sewers, the Garden State has more sludge with less space for disposal than any other in the union. The 230,000 dry tons per year of sludge produced now are expected to double by 1990.

The Atlantic Ocean was the dumping site for the sludge generated by 66 percent of New Jersey residents. By 1976 the practice was causing all sorts of headaches and other disorders. Floating trash washed up on beaches, and fish kills were often reported. The State of Maryland sued Camden to force that city to stop dumping sludge 40 miles off its shoreline. And then came passage of the federal legislation to ban sludge dumping by 1981.

With that history, one can appreciate how timely it was that in May 1978 a sludge-composting plant began operations in Camden. The $2.2-million compost facility involves dewatering the sludge, mixing sludge with a bulking agent such as wood chips, and aerating the mounds of sludge on a large cement slab during a 21-day "pasteurization" period. The wood chips are then screened out for reuse and the compost is stabilized for another 30 days. Then the compost is ready for use as a soil conditioner. Other bulking materials being considered are municipal and commercial solid wastes, agricultural wastes (like corn stover), food-processing industry wastes, and other materials such as shredded tires.

The Camden Composting Project involves six units of the Agricultural Experiment Station at Rutgers University's Cook College, with 13 individual projects organized under the program. The Department of Soils and Crops is investigating a variety of uses and applications for compost on New Jersey soils. The Department of Environmental Sciences is studying pathogen-destruction composting of industrial wastes and leachate control. The Department of Agricultural Economics and Marketing is looking at costs and compost markets. Also involved are the Departments of Biochemistry and Microbiology, Agricultural Engineering, and Environmental Resources.

Professor Singley and his colleagues point out that because of high levels of heavy metals in New Jersey sludges as a result of industrial discharge that is not pretreated, the finished compost will not be utilized in food production. But nonfood areas could include golf courses, nurseries, turfgrass farms, cemeteries, greenhouses, playgrounds, highway strips, and military installations. Other areas include landfill cover, strip-mined lands, and sand and gravel pits.

A Brief History of Recycling Wastes on the Farm*

Joel A. Tarr, professor of history and urban affairs at Carnegie-Mellon University in Pittsburgh, has done considerable research into America's agricultural heritage of waste utilization. He begins a report, "From City to Farm: Urban Wastes and the American Farmer" (published in *Agricultural History*, volume 17, 1975), with this quotation from a speech given to the Suffolk, Massachusetts, Medical Society in 1884:

> A great city is the most powerful of stercovaries [toilets or places to store manure]. To employ the city to enrich the plains would be a sure success. But the filth is swept into the abyss. All the human and animal manure which the world loses, restored to the land instead of being thrown into the water, would suffice to nourish the world. These heaps of garbage at the corners of the stone blocks, these tumbrils of mire, jolting the streets at night, these horrid scavengers' carts, these fetid streams of subterranean slime which

*Professor Tarr and colleagues at Carnegie Mellon University have published a comprehensive study of this subject in a 1977 publication, *Retrospective Assessment of Wastewater Technology in the United States: 1800-1972.*

the pavement hides, what is all this? It is the flourishing meadow, the green grass, the thyme and sage; it is game, it is cattle, hay, corn, bread upon the table, warm blood in the veins.

—Dr. Henry J. Barnes

Professor Tarr notes that throughout the 1800s and into the early 1900s farmers and scavengers collected human wastes from urban cesspools and privy vaults, then used them to fertilize a wide variety of crops:

Such a practice was the natural result of a sewerless society, one that did not make use of water to remove human wastes, and one that believed that those wastes had an economic value. In some cases, farmers themselves collected the wastes, often paying for the privilege....

In some cities, the wastes were first mixed with earth and other materials, and the mixture applied to the land or sold to processing plants to be manufactured into fertilizer. This latter practice was followed in eight cities, including New York, Baltimore, Cleveland, and Washington, D.C. The fertilizer was usually marketed under the trade name of "Poudrette," and advertisements boasting of its value on lawns, garden vegetables, corn, potatoes, and tobacco appeared in farm journals as early as 1839.

In most cities, however, the wastes were applied directly to the land, although with certain restrictions. The law often stipulated that cesspools and privy vaults could be emptied only at night and prohibited the use of night soil on farms within the gathering ground of the city's water supply. Usually the privies were emptied by buckets, and the contents taken away in horse-drawn night-soil carts. By 1880, 11 cities had adopted the "odorless evacuator"—a vacuum pump powered by hand or by steam which destroyed objectionable gases as removal took place.

Precise information about the volume of human wastes used for agriculture is rare. There is information available, however, for a few cities. In 1880, for instance, Brooklyn reported that 20,000 cubic feet of night soil were taken each year from the city's 25,000 privy vaults and applied to "farms and gardens outside the city." In the same year, Philadelphia estimated that its 20 "odorless vault-emptying companies removed about 22,000 tons of fluid matter per year," and that "the matters removed are largely used by farmers and market gardeners of the vicinity." Urban night soil was not frequently spread as fertilizer on truck farms, orchards, and vineyards within a few miles of the city where it was collected.

Baltimore fertilized garden crops with urban night soil as late as the first decade of the twentieth century. The city was without a system of municipal sewers until 1912, and human wastes were deposited in over 70,000 cesspools with privy vaults. "Night-soil" men, using either odorless excavators or buckets, emptied the vaults and sold the contents to a contractor for 25 cents per load of 200 gallons. The contractor shipped the wastes by barge to a depot ten miles below the city and sold them to farmers. Virginia and Maryland farmers bought over 12 million gallons of Baltimore wastes a year and used it to grow crops such as cabbage, kale, spinach, potatoes, and tomatoes. These crops were then sold in the Baltimore market. According to one reference, "little smell" arose from either the pits where the fertilizing material was stored or the lands to which it was applied.

Baltimore was unusual in that it was the only major city in the nation that continued to recycle its wastes on neighboring farms into the twentieth century. The disappearance of the agricultural use of urban wastes resulted primarily from three factors: increases in urban population, changes in technology, and increasing concern with public health.

By the Civil War, the system of having scavengers and farmers empty urban cesspools was proving increasingly inefficient, due mainly to rampant urban growth. As cities became more densely populated and urban slums proliferated, cesspools proved incapable of handling the increased loads of human wastes. The very areas of the cities that needed the most attention from city scavenging departments—the densely packed slums—were neglected. There had always been complaints about the imperfections of the system, and now its deficiencies were amplified. Health Departments and sanitarians began to demand that water closets and water carriage systems for removing human wastes be installed throughout the cities.

The second factor disrupting the scavenger–cesspool system was a technology that in itself was considered of great benefit to cities: the installation of piped-in water supplies. By 1860, the 12 largest cities in the nation, as well as a number of smaller ones, had introduced running water, installed primarily because of the pollution of local water sources and the need for large quantities of water for fire-fighting.

The introduction of piped-in water to cities greatly increased water consumption. In 1858, for example, cities with piped-in water, like Philadelphia and Boston, were consuming 40 to 60 gallons of water a day per capita. This was a vast increase over the estimated consumption of three gallons a day for cities without piped-in water. In the absence of sewers, this water was diverted to the cesspools or into street gutters.

The scavenger–cesspool system of waste collection faded before the widespread adoption of water closets. Sometimes these water closets were connected (often illegally) to existing storm sewers, but more often they were run into the cesspools.

The cesspools proved incapable of handling the resulting flood. Citizens who were used to having their cesspools emptied once or twice a year now found themselves forced to pay for cleaning every month. In addition, the cesspools often overflowed, threatening health and offending the senses. Urban residents soon demanded sewers to handle household and human wastes.

The last factor in the abandonment of the scavenger–cesspool system and the substitution of sewers and water closets was dread of cholera and yellow fever epidemics that swept American cities periodically throughout much of the nineteenth century, along with rising death rates from diseases such as typhoid and infant diarrhea. By the 1870s and 1880s, this concern became a crusade uniting public health officials, physicians, and sanitary engineers. Some members of the sanitary crusade believed that cesspools and privies gave off "miasmas" that spread disease while others accepted the new germ theory. Regardless of which medical theory they accepted, most in the crusade believed that cities should build sewerage and require water closets to remove human and household wastes.

By the 1880s, most large and many small American cities were building or planning to build sewerage. Simultaneously, increasing numbers of people adopted water closets and water consumption increased. A few sanitarians, whose voices were overwhelmed, argued that the water closet and water carriage system wasted the valuable materials in human wastes, and they urged adoption of such alternatives as the earth closet or pail system, both of which were widely used in Europe.

During the last decades of the nineteenth century and the first decade of the twentieth, American cities made vast expenditures on sewerage. In 1890, cities with an aggregate population of 14,711,117 were served by 8,199 miles of sewers, or 1,795 persons per mile; by 1909, 20,593,303 people lived in cities with sewers but the miles of sewer had increased to 24,972, or 825 persons per mile. As miles of sewers increased, so did miles of water main and the number of water closets adopted. A new system of waste removal had appeared to take the place of the scavenger-cesspool, but the old problem of the ultimate disposal of the wastes still remained—and still remains to this day.

The scavenger-cesspool system, despite its imperfections, made it possible to recycle human wastes. With the advent of the water carriage system, most cities dumped their sewage in neighboring streams and rivers, creating serious pollution problems, although some cities did experiment with sewer farms. Downstream cities drew their water supplies from the rivers in which upstream cities dumped their sewage. Nowadays we treat raw sewage to reduce the threat to the public health, but after treatment, most sludge is still wasted and is still creating pollution.

Even the most ardent recyclers do not advocate returning to the "good old days" when raw sludge was returned to farmland in a manner described by Professor Tarr. What recyclers do advocate is the controlled recycling of properly treated wastes for the production of food and fiber, and for optimum restoration of soil fertility.

Clarence Golueke, research biologist at the University of California and senior editor of *Compost Science/Land Utilization*, sees large-scale composting as having "attained a level of prominence surpassing that attained in its heyday in the late forties and early fifties":

> Even more interesting is the fact that high hopes in the utilization
> of the process are held by individuals who hitherto saw little utility
> in it with respect to any municipal-scale operation. The reasons for
> the turn-about in attitude do not spring from any great interest in
> conservation or concern for the environment. Rather, like the usual
> motivation in modern society, the reasons are ultimately traceable
> to economics.

Interestingly, composting—the age-old favorite practice of gardeners the world over because it recycles nutrients back to the land—is now seen as the cheapest acceptable technique for many city and industrial organic wastes. And America's gardeners, nurserymen, and landscapers provide a tremendous demand for locally processed wastes. For example, the Energy Resource Company of Cambridge, Massachusetts, recently did a marketing study for the Metropolitan District Commission of Boston on sludge compost produced at the Deer Island treatment plant. The product is called Metroloam, and the people at Energy Resource Company (ERCO) were amazed at its popularity among greenhouse and nursery operators, city parks personnel, and landscapers; one nursery wanted more than a month's total output.

"I am not saying that the sludge is better than fertilizer, but under the conditions of this experiment, it did a better job," Dr. William E. Larson, research soil scientist at the University of Minnesota, recently reported at a conference called "Land Application of Municipal Wastes." While the nation and the world run short of fertilizer for croplands, we waste more than 350,000 tons of potential fertilizer annually. The figures break down roughly this way:

215,000 tons of nitrogen
150,000 tons of phosphorus
15,000 tons of potassium

These amounts of major plant nutrients are contained in sludge from the sewage treatment plants across the nation. Dr. Larson's research illustrated how sludges boosted the yield of field corn and potatoes grown on an infertile sandy soil in Minnesota. Crop response was usually related to the nitrogen- and phosphorus-supplying capacity of the sludge, the nutrient status of the soil, and the nutrient requirements of the crop.

Other researchers have also found positive benefits from sludge recycling onto land. Here are highlights of some recent study results:

Growing two crops of forest seedlings from one application of screened composted sludge: F. R. Gouin of the University of Maryland's Department of Horticulture successfully discovered the optimum rates when applying treated wastes to growing seedlings of flowering dogwoods, tulip, and maple trees.

Optimum use of sewage sludge on agricultural land: "We are trying to find ways to obtain the maximum benefits and at the same time decrease the problems involved with the use of sewage sludge on farmland," writes soils professor Roscoe Ellis, Jr., of Kansas State University.

Soil management systems and productivity of vegetable crops: Frank Eggert, professor of horticulture at the University of Maine, has incorporated composted sludge from the Bangor project into his test plots.

Agricultural value of irradiated sludge: In a project that combines high and low technology, Professor Mary Beth Kirkham of Oklahoma State University is studying the effect of irradiation to kill unwanted pathogens and noting the outcome on trace elements in the sludge.

Soil and environmental chemistry program: A research program directed by Dale Baker, a Pennsylvania State University agronomy professor, tests sludge, soil, and plant samples "to determine accurately the type and amount of nutrient material

Forced mechanical aeration by pumping air through perforated pipes leading into the piles of mixed materials provides the necessary process control to produce hygienically acceptable end products.

necessary to reach optimum levels for crop growth." A service lab has been set up which analyzes sludge and soil samples on a routine basis for Pennsylvania residents.

Soil properties affecting absorption of heavy metals from waste materials: Sixteen soil samples collected throughout the northeastern U.S. are having their chemical and physical properties analyzed in relation to heavy-metal absorption. This work is being conducted in several northeastern states, and coordinated at the University of Maryland.

Reclaiming strip-mine spoils: Both the University of Kentucky and Pennsylvania State University are conducting extensive investigations into the use of waste materials for strip-mine revegetation. In Pennsylvania alone there are more than 300,000 acres which were strip-mined before enactment of the 1971 Surface Mining Conservation and Reclamation Act. These acres remain barren, continue to erode, and produce large quantities of acid runoff. Researchers at Penn State took on the challenge of revegetating these areas. Professors William Sopper and Louis Kardos have great confidence

Durham, New Hampshire, composts approximately 40 to 50 tons per week of raw, dewatered, primary sludge. Recently, Durham has constructed a facility which makes the composting process even more economical and efficient.

in the restorative ability of city wastes following their "living filter" experiments with spraying forests with effluent. The results indicated that effluent and sludge treatments of strip-mine spoils have significant beneficial effects.

A screening device is used at Bangor, Maine, to separate wood chips from the finished compost. Wood chips help to aerate the composting materials.

One example of the many uses for composted sludge
—landscaping along highways near Durham, New
Hampshire.

Producing and marketing compost: Bangor, Maine, is composting its entire sludge production. According to R. Kent Anderson of
the EPA's Systems Management Division, "the city's experience in
selling screened compost was very favorable. About half went to
private individuals for use on flower beds and lawns, while the rest
was sold to other city departments and park development projects,
and used as loam substitutes to reestablish grass along esplanades."

Farm crop production with wastes in the Northwest: In
Oregon's Willamette Valley, sludge from the cities of Portland,
Salem, and Aloha has been applied to sweet corn, wheat, and tall
fescue to assay effect on crop yields. A smaller project is directed
toward the agricultural utilization of tannery waste material.

Turfgrass production: At the Rhode Island Agricultural Experiment Station, four years of research have been conducted on land

applications of industrial fermentation wastes to determine their effects on potato and turfgrass production.

Beautifying urban areas and creating parks: Constitution Gardens, a park created especially for the Bicentennial in Washington, D.C., consists of 42 acres near the Lincoln Memorial. The U.S. Park Service saved $200,000 in fertilizer costs by using 9,000 tons of composted sludge.

Distribution and Marketing of Sludge and Wastewater

Cities, villages, and treatment-plant operators and companies have devised many ways to distribute and market sludge. Some give it away for free while others bag and sell it. Sometimes it's composted and sold by a private company. Other times, local farmers haul it away as a favor to the manager of the treatment facility.

In Chicago, the overriding concern is to "recycle rather than destroy" solids which are produced at the Metropolitan Sanitary District's treatment plants. The volume is so great that the city wants to distribute all of it, not sell only a small fraction. Hence Chicago's Nu-Earth uses a program of free delivery which costs the district much less than any of the other methods available.

Within specified delivery areas, large-scale users can receive truckloads. There are also several distribution points within the district boundaries so users don't have far to go in order to pick up a supply.

The Milwaukee Sewerage Commission has effectively developed a nationwide marketing program for its granular activated sewage sludge Milorganite. "We still sell everything we produce—about 80,000 tons yearly," reports C. G. Wilson, sales manager and head agronomist of the Milwaukee commission.

Available in every state, Milorganite is used extensively on golf courses, lawns, and city parks as well as gardens and orchards. It is packaged in 50-pound bags and has been on the market for more than 40 years.

One of the best examples of a private company marketing sludge is provided by Clay Kellogg, whose firm has a contract with Los Angeles County. "With a well-digested composted sewage with volatile acids below the detection range of ten parts per million, you have the finest product available to sell," says Kellogg.

One of the most interesting examples of sludge utilization exists in the area of Braunschweig, Germany. Braunschweig has a

The Northglenn, Colorado, Water Management System—using wastewater to enrich farm soils.

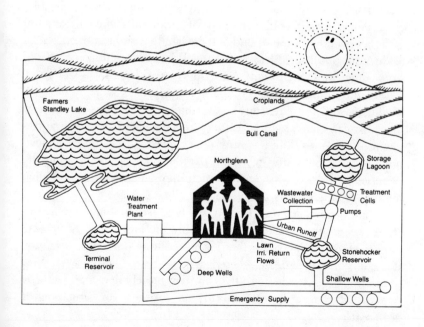

population of 380,000 and a long history of utilizing sludge on farmland. The following information was prepared by an internationally known soil scientist, Dr. Cord Tietjen, of the Braunschweig Agricultural Station:

> Twenty years ago, the Braunschweig Sewage Utilization was founded by a union of the city of Braunschweig with 550 farmers, and an area of more than 10,000 acres, where the sewage is being finally and completely disposed of and utilized in crop farming. The Braunschweig Sewage Utilization Association is demonstrating with regard to aspects of environmental protection that remarkable efficiency is obtainable through sewage land treatment by coordinating sanitary engineering, water resources policy, and agriculture, where the soil and climatic conditions are favorable, and the farmers' economic situation can be improved.

There is nearly no sludge produced in this kind of sewage treatment, contrary to the procedure in complicated sewage-treatment plants. The higher the purification efficiency, the greater is the mass and volume of sludge to be handled and removed, and—aside from public health aspects—this also increases the problems of processing and transportation for the final disposal.

In this country, some comparable projects exist in Muskegon, Michigan, and most recently in Northglenn, Colorado. In this city located near Denver, an agreement was arranged between Northglenn officials needing a freshwater supply and a farmers' association seeking nutrients in water for their cropland. A mutually beneficial contract was signed which may well serve as a recyling model for other areas of the nation.

The Northglenn plan is designed to satisfy municipal demands while keeping agricultural land in production. The system will divert water owned by the Farmers Reservoir and Irrigation Company to Northglenn, where it will be treated and delivered for domestic use. Afterward, the nutrient-enriched water will be treated, stored, and returned to the farmers for irrigation of croplands.

7

Garbage Fit for Energy— and Fertilizer

In mid-1978, a high-ranking official at the World Trade Center in New York declared that he'd like to have access to all the garbage in the city. He would burn all this garbage for fuel to create energy to bring more industry into Manhattan.

About six years before, an official in New York's city hall also envisioned a total solution to urban garbage. His plan was to reclaim Pennsylvania's strip mines with New York City garbage, which— according to his analysis—would be so effective that Pennsylvanians would want to dig up previously landfilled garbage for shipment.

All or nothing—either all good or all bad. Such has been the official, and unofficial, view of garbage. Meanwhile garbage collection and disposal use up billions of tax dollars and poor practices cause major health and environmental problems. Realistic recycling of garbage cannot be an all-or-nothing proposition, nor can we affort to tolerate the dump-and-forget attitude any longer.

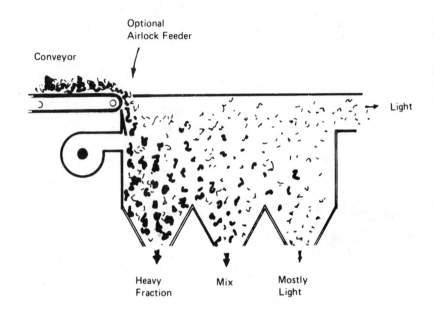

Optional
Airlock Feeder

Conveyor

Light

Heavy
Fraction

Mix

Mostly
Light

This horizontal air classifier, developed by the U.S.
Bureau of Mines, is an example of technology needed
in refuse-derived-fuel installations.

Garbage as Fuel

Hempstead, New York, opened up a waste-into-energy facility
in mid-1978. A $73-million, 2,000-ton-per-day facility, the design is a
scaled-up version of the Black Clawson plant in Franklin, Ohio,
where garbage is fed into "hydrapulpers" and material is salvaged.
In Hempstead, the original forecast when the plant opened was that
15 percent of the community's residential electricity load would be
produced.

The Hempstead plant was about the tenth such facility to
develop in the United States; some are demonstration projects,
while others are full scale, using various technologies developed by

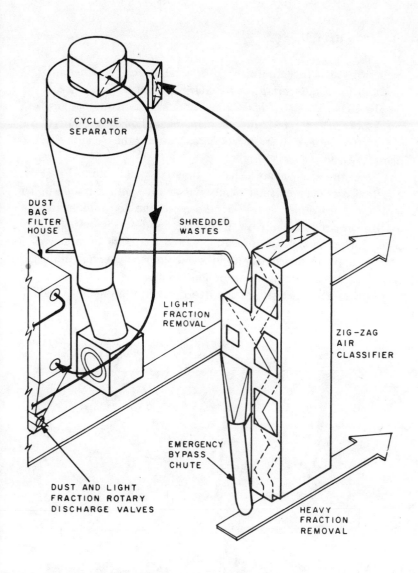

CYCLONE
SEPARATOR

DUST
BAG
FILTER
HOUSE

SHREDDED
WASTES

LIGHT
FRACTION
REMOVAL

ZIG−ZAG
AIR
CLASSIFIER

EMERGENCY
BYPASS
CHUTE

DUST AND LIGHT
FRACTION ROTARY
DISCHARGE VALVES

HEAVY
FRACTION
REMOVAL

Configuration of the air classification chambers varies among
manufacturers. This vertical zig-zag classifier illustrates one
approach. *(courtesy National Center for Resource Recovery, Inc.)*

such firms as Wheelabrator-Frye, American Can, Raytheon, UOP, Combustion Engineering, and Black Clawson.

In Massachusetts, 1,500 tons of garbage from Saugus and nearby towns enter a $45-million plant located on the grounds of the old landfill dump and are turned into steam for the General Electric plant in Lynn.

One financial analyst has estimated that within 10 years, resource recovery in such plants will evolve into a billion-dollar industry, with about 30 to 50 percent of the 150 million tons of garbage created annually being converted into fuel in more than 100 plants. The plants, he forecasts, would generate as much as 5 percent of the electricity for utilities and almost 20 percent of the gas requirements in certain metropolitan areas.

Others caution against such overoptimistic projections, calling

Black Clawson put its Hydrasposal system to use in Middletown, Ohio.

Hydrasposal ™
Solid Waste Disposal System

the process "unproven," citing problems in such plants and the low costs of landfilling where cities are still able to do so, and warning that one explosion can be expected for every 20,000 tons of garbage shredded.

In a Worldwatch Institute study on recycling, "Moving Toward a Sustainable Society," author Denis Hayes records these objections from critics of resource-recovery plants:

> Proponents of source separation feel that centralized facilities are capital-intensive behemoths that produce little net energy and recover a comparatively small fraction of the material value of trash. Resource recovery centers are viewed by this group as marginally better than landfills as a destination for whatever is not successfully recovered through source separation. But there is a strong fear that economies of scale will dictate that huge units be built at high expense to handle the entire current volume of urban waste. Afterward, cities would have a strong vested interest in maintaining the same level of waste in order to maximize the return on their sunk investments. This could lead to official discouragement—or even forbidding—of community recycling schemes.

As noted elsewhere, you don't have to be a dedicated environmentalist to be skeptical or critical of the grand garbage-to-fuel schemes. Executives with companies that are producing the equipment and systems doubt if the economics will ever be right, and question their colleagues who are pushing an "unproven" process so hard.

Pyrolysis is one of the methods being advanced to convert wastes into liquid, gaseous, and solid fuels—but it has not been successfully used on a commercial scale. Pyrolysis is defined as the thermal decomposition of an organic material without oxygen, at temperatures usually starting near 600–700°F.

But support for garbage-to-fuel facilities mounts as energy reserves dwindle and prices mount. In New York State, for example, environmental conservation commissioner Peter Berle has proposed that his state commit itself to convert most of its garbage to fuel for power-generating plants, after magnetically separating useful metals.

According to figures released by the National Center for Resource Recovery, Inc., of Washington, D.C., the scorecard of such resource-recovery plants as of early 1978 range from small, modular combustion units with heat recovery to intermediate-sized plants such as the facilities in Ames, Iowa, Franklin, Ohio, and Nashville, Tennessee. The large mass-burning plants producing steam from 1,000 or more tons of garbage per day were located in Saugus, Massachusetts, and in Hempstead, New York. Others are scheduled for Baltimore, Chicago, Milwaukee, New Orleans, and San Diego. In Pompano Beach, Florida, a demonstration project for recovering methane gas from solid waste and sewage sludge has begun operations.

Under the system for generating refuse-derived fuel (RDF), trash is first shredded. The next step is to separate mechanically (or by aeration techniques) the heavy metals and glass from paper and plastics. The heavy material is available for sale to secondary-materials dealers. The light material (the RDF) is available for burning.

In the early 1970s Middletown, Ohio, began using equipment which had long been used in the pulping and papermaking industry to convert its refuse into such useful products as paper fiber, ferrous metals, and glass cullet. A hydrapulper made by the Black Clawson Company is the heart of the system. In it, all pulpable, grindable, and friable materials (such as food waste, paper, plastic, rubber, glass, wood, and leaves) are disintegrated and removed through an internal screen as a water slurry.

The slurry is then pumped through a unit that removes broken glass, sand, and bits of metal larger than one-eighth of an inch. The next step is to extract fiber for reuse as paper products.

A 2,000-ton-per-day municipal- and industrial-waste resource-recovery facility is being developed in Pinellas County, Florida.

Solid waste from Pinellas communities will be processed in the facility using combustion technology developed in Germany. This technology is in large-scale, commercial operation in about 15 countries.

The resource-recovery facility will use a 40-megawatt turbine generator to produce about 500 kilowatt-hours of electricity per ton of processed refuse and transmit it to the Florida Power Corporation. Sale of electricity will be the principal source of resource-recovery revenue to the county.

The Pinellas County plant will be built by UOP, Inc., which also operates a similar plant near North Andover, Massachusetts.

In a study of "Energy Production from Municipal Wastes," Donald L. Klass of the Institute of Gas Technology in Chicago has calculated that the heating value of municipal solid waste (MSW) is about 3,000 to 7,000 BTUs per pound received. (His "typical MSW" contains about 15–35 percent moisture by weight, 40–70 percent organic components, and 10–20 percent inorganic components.)

Concerning particle size reduction to prepare material for direct fuel use, Dr. Klass notes that the size of the material influences the rate at which the gasification process occurs. He also points out that co-combustion of RDF with coal has recently been started in full-scale systems, permitting RDF to be used in large existing electric power plants.

Garbage into Fertilizer and Soil Conditioner

In July 1978 Key West, Florida, announced that a $1,740,500 contract had been awarded to the Fairfield Engineering Company of Marion, Ohio, for construction of a 50-ton-per-day compost plant. The Key West plant will use the same process employed in Altoona, Pennsylvania. Since 1951, Altoona has been composting its city garbage. After grinding, wet pulping, and dewatering, the material is fed into a circular digester. Stirring is done by augers suspended from a rotating bridge in the circular tank.

Originally, the city of Altoona signed a 10-year contract with Altoona Farm, Inc., a group of businessmen, at an annual fee of $42,000 and a rent-free lease for the old incinerator building. City garbage—25 tons daily—is delivered to the site.

The plant, now operated by the Fairfield Engineering Company, produces compost which is sold in six markets:

1.	Lightweight fertilizer carrier	26%
2.	Poultry litter	44%
3.	Land restoration	14%
4.	Bagged soil conditioner	3%
5.	Nursery	8%
6.	Miscellaneous	5%

Composting municipal wastes has had a mixed record in this country, but then no process—whether it be incineration, refuse-derived fuel, dumping, or landfill—has a better record. There are nontechnical, usually nonquantifiable, factors involved in any solid-waste management program that stresses recycling, and certainly composting in particular. These factors can be classified as institutional, political, and human, and are as important as the technological aspects of any specific process.

These nontechnical factors include the ability of officials, citizens, and organizations in a given area to work together to make a recycling plan work. Cooperation is needed between public works and parks agencies, professional consultants and concerned lay people, private sector and public sector, urban areas and rural areas.

Officials need to be elected who are committed to the success of a solid-waste management plan based on converting wastes into a well-used resource *if a recycling solution is wanted*. That's where politics play a most significant role.

Neither the public nor elected officials should be misled into

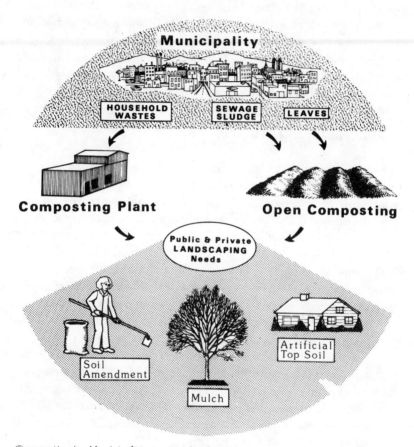

Municipality

HOUSEHOLD WASTES   SEWAGE SLUDGE   LEAVES

Composting Plant   **Open Composting**

Public & Private LANDSCAPING Needs

Soil Amendment

Mulch

Artificial Top Soil

Composting for Municipalities, as seen by the New York State Department of Agricultural Engineering at Cornell University.

thinking that there is a utopian solution that will see today's wastes be tomorrow's gold mine. Time and again (this specifically applies to the history of composting in the United States), when unrealistic expectations or promises were made, wastes continue to be a burden. Garbage to gold—a fine slogan, but totally unrealistic.

Garbage to a resource—that is completely attainable, and composting is one significant way to achieve that objective.

The Composting Process

Since composting is a biological process, the value of a compost system can be judged by the extent to which it provides optimum conditions for biological reactions within the constraints of economic feasibility. As far as composting is concerned, the more important conditions to be provided at optimum levels are oxygen supply (aeration), moisture content, and bacterial nutrients. The latter must be present in adequate amount and in proper proportions. Moisture content and oxygen content are influenced primarily by system design, whereas bacterial nutrient supply and balance are almost solely functions of the wastes themselves.

Because modern composting is an aerobic process, the smaller the oxygen deficit, the more satisfactory is the progress of the process. Aerobic composting is characterized by the attainment of high temperatures (55° to 70°C), is generally free of vile odors, and is more rapid than anaerobic composting. The high temperatures have an important role in killing pathogens, and hence in the production of a safe product. Moreover, according to Dr. Clarence Golueke of the University of California, many researchers are of the opinion that decomposition proceeds more rapidly at high temperatures. While a system need not provide heat input, it should be designed to prevent heat loss, at least enough to allow a buildup of heat within the composting mass. Maintaining the proper moisture content involves adding water when the moisture content is too low or removing it when the content is excessively high. The former is readily accomplished; the latter, with some difficulty. For reasons of economics, the usual approach is to step up the rate of aeration, and thereby the rate of evaporation.

To be effective, a compost system must consistently yield a satisfactory product. As Dr. Golueke notes:

> Unreliability with compost plants not only can be a result of poor design, but it also can be the consequence of underdesign. Unfortunately, the latter often occurs with mechanical compost systems and generally is the outcome of an attempt to make capital costs more palatable. *A good rule of thumb is that the simpler a system is, the greater is its reliability.*
>
> It is in the area of economics that the greatest care must be taken when evaluating a compost system. Inasmuch as costs, both

This aerial view of a composting plant in Europe shows the ramp and receiving apron, biostablizers for composting, screening house, windrow areas, and bagging shed.

capital and operational, usually are key factors in the decision of a community shopping for a compost system, the tendency is for entrepreneurs to understate costs in the two areas. Capital costs are hard to conceal, but they can be softened by offering underdesigned equipment or by overstating the true capacity of the equipment. The penalty, as far as the unsuspecting buyer is concerned, is, of course, costly and frequent downtime and accumulations of backlogged wastes. Overstating the capacity is done by claiming unrealistically short retention times, hence...the need to check the product of an existing plant. On the average, capital costs per ton of material processed with mechanized systems are comparable to those for incineration.

Most designs of existing systems concentrate on providing aeration, by either agitation or injection. The emphasis on aeration stems from the fact that it has been repeatedly demonstrated that oxygen availability is the predominant limiting factor in rate of composting.

Compost systems are generally divided into two broad types—windrow (open) and closed (mechanical). "Closed" and "mechanical" are terms applied to those systems which depend on the containment of the composting material in a specially designed unit (reactor, digester), at least in the initial stages of the compost process. Because of the high capital cost involved, the volume capacity of the compost units must be kept low, the units are designed to permit only brief retention periods, and reliance is made on windrowing to complete the process. In windrow systems, the material to be composted is stacked in windrows immediately without undergoing treatment in an enclosed reactor (the word "open" is often used because no reactor is involved, but it does not preclude sheltering the windrows during the active stage of composting). The term "windrow" as applied to composting processes should not be construed as an antonym of "mechanical" or "mechanized" because modern, large-scale composting does involve varying degrees of mechanization, although largely in the form of the equipment used to turn over the compost for aeration purposes.

Each type has its advantages and disadvantages. Closed systems have the advantage of closer control than is possible with windrow composting. This control applies both to the microbial environment in the composting mass and to emissions from it. With respect to environmental control, it means that favorable conditions can be provided or emphasized and unfavorable conditions lessened, or in some cases excluded. Emission control minimizes unfavorable impact on the environment external to the reactor. For example, bad odors can be trapped and treated. This capability is very important, inasmuch as in the brief history of municipal composting in this country every operation at one time or another has incurred the wrath of its neighbors, mostly because of a bad odor situation. Conventional means do exist for preventing the release of foul odors from a plant. Another advantage of closed composting is that the process is protected from adverse climatic conditions during its critical, active phase.

The prime advantage of windrow systems as compared to closed systems is that their capital costs are much less, although their operational costs may be comparable to those of closed systems.

SOME CLOSED SYSTEMS

The following descriptions give some general idea of the types of composting systems available. They are based on data contained in a report prepared by G. M. Wesner of the consulting engineering firm Culp/Wesner/Culp, as well as information supplied by Dr. Clarence Golueke and the manufacturers.

The Fairfield digester, (manufactured by the Fairfield Engineering Co., Marion, Ohio 43302) is a circular vessel. Aerator augers are suspended from a bridge that travels around the top of the digester wall. Integral units of the bridge include: the drive machinery to rotate the bridge, the machinery for the multiple

The Metro Composting system—in action.

aerator augers, and a conveyor which transports incoming material from an overhead center hopper to the place where it enters the digester near the wall. The material is aerated and moved toward the center discharge by the action of the multiple augers. A conveyor at the bottom of the digester removes digested material. Air is forced into the digester by a motor-driven blower and distributed throughout the material by pipes.

A self-generated temperature of approximately 150°F is produced and maintained by the metabolism of the aerobic-thermophilic microorganisms multiplying within the waste material.

The Fairfield digester at Altoona is 38 feet in diameter and, with a depth of material of 6 feet, has a capacity of 25 tons per day of organic input containing 58 percent moisture and weighing 30 pounds per cubic foot. The digester is totally enclosed, with air pipes in the bottom which receive forced air from the plenum chamber by means of motor valves that are operated automatically from temperature and oxygen probes located in the bottom of the digester. The digester is of the continuous-flow type so that digested material, having been retained in the digester approximately seven days, is automatically discharged as new material is introduced.

The Metro Waste Composting system is sold by Resource Conversion Systems, Inc. (Houston, Texas 77024). The system is relatively simple in design and incorporates both forced aeration and tumbling. "Ballpark" estimates in 1978 dollars quoted by the vendor for a plant to compost sludge are $500,000 for a 5-dry-ton-per-day plant to $2,000,000 for a 100-dry-ton-per-day plant. Direct operating and maintenance costs, exclusive of amortization and

The Brown Bear composting auger (12 feet wide, 40 inches in diameter) operates on windrow piles.

A rotating drum equipped with shredding teeth
processes material in the Cobey composting machine.

purchase of external bulking material, are about $20 to less than $5
per dry ton for the 5- and 100-dry-ton-per-day plants.

WINDROW SYSTEMS

The biggest development in windrow-system technology in
recent years has been the proliferation of different types of
mechanical turning equipment and refinements in forced aeration
developed by the USDA at Beltsville, Maryland, Durham, New
Hampshire, and Bangor, Maine. The turning equipment ranges from
the relatively simple in design to the complex. Some was developed
specifically for composting, e.g., "Aerobe" (Aenco, Inc., New
Castle, Delaware 19720), "Scarab" (Scarab Manufacturing & Leas-

ing, Inc., White Deer, Texas 79097), and the "Cobey Composter" (a division of Eagle Crusher Co., Inc., Route 2, Box 72, Galion, Ohio), while others are minor adaptations of machines originally designed for other uses, e.g., "Brown Bear" (Roscoe Brown, Inc., Lenox, Iowa 50851).

Typically, turning machines are designed to pick up the composting material and redeposit it. Differences between designs are in the manner in which the picking up and redepositing are accomplished, and in the position of the reconstructed pile, that is, whether the latter is alongside or in the position of the original pile. In both cases, the machine moves head-on into the pile, but in one

Compost at the Bronx (New York) Project is made from 500 cubic yards per week of vegetable waste generated by the Hunt's Point Produce Market.

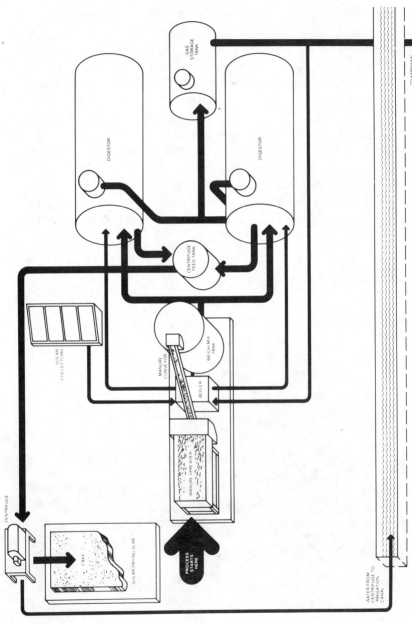

IMPERIAL VALLEY BIOGAS PROJECT

The biogas test facility utilizes solar collector panels
(left) that gather energy from the sun for process heat.
Fermented residue is placed on a solar drying slab
(foreground) to dry thoroughly before being mixed
with grain.

Left. The Imperial Valley Biogas Project. This diagram illustrates the biogas
(methane and carbon dioxide) production process. A mixture of cattle manure and
water is held in two digestor tanks for fermentation. Solar panels are used to maintain
the digestors at the correct temperature. The biogas is collected in a storage tank until
needed. Fermented residue from the digestors is piped through a feed tank and then
dehydrated in the centrifuge. The residue is dried on a solar slab before mixing with
normal cattle feed.

case the material is deposited alongside the machine and in the second, behind the machine. With one type, the processing component consists of a rotating drum equipped with shredding teeth ("Cobey Composter"), while with another, the agitation is accomplished with an auger ("Brown Bear").

Composting in a Social Context

Demolition goes on daily in the South Bronx section of New York City. Empty shells of buildings stretch for miles, and there are more than 250 acres of vacant land. In June 1978, a composting project began near Hunt's Point, a major wholesale distribution area for fresh fruits and vegetables in the South Bronx. Miranda Smith of the National Center for Appropriate Technology wrote this description of that project:

> Composting is mostly viewed as a solution to waste management problems and as a method of improving soil quality. However, it should also be considered in a social context. Composting is a response and a solution to some of our most pressing urban revitalization problems. The people who form the Bronx Frontier Development Corporation are using compost as the key element in a project to revitalize the South Bronx of New York.

In the eyes of community development workers, the composting project offered a way to revitalize the spirit as well as the physical environment. Using the compost, some lots could be turned into parks; in other spaces vegetables could be grown, helping local residents cut food costs and improve their diets. The Bronx Frontier Development Corporation, led by Irma Fleck and Jack Flanagan, is using the compost process as a key strategy for greening the South Bronx. Compost is now being made from vegetable and fruit wastes, from leaves from a neighboring community, and from manure from horse stables within the city.

Biogasification for Energy Creation and Food Production

When wastes such as manures from farm animals or urban garbage are stabilized through biological activity in the absence of atmospheric oxygen, methane (CH_4) is produced. Thus, anaerobic digestion is the basic principle in the biogasification process.

The history of anaerobic digestion in the treatment of wastes practically parallels that of wastewater treatment, since it is used to stabilize the sludges produced in the treatment process. However, in its first stages of technology, anaerobic digestion was rather primitive and took the form more of a "holding" tank than of a unit designed to control and facilitate the fermentation process, as are modern digesters.

The anaerobic digestion of farm wastes also has a relatively long history, but it was never practiced on a scale of any magnitude. It was used on a few farms in France and Germany during World Wars I and II, not so much as a waste-treatment device, but rather to produce the combustible gas methane as a fuel for household cooking.

During the past 30 to 40 years, such methane digesters have come into widespread use in rural India; estimates place the number at almost 2,000. In the Indian application, both human as well as animal excreta are digested.

Biogasification is considered to be a promising solution for supplemental energy at the village level in Sub-Saharan Africa. In its report *Energy for the Villages of Africa*, the Overseas Development Council rates the technology of biogasification as "known and reliable, particularly where livestock are abundant."

Biogas technology and utilization receive much attention in China, whose organic waste recycling practices are documented in a study by the Food and Agricultural Organization of the United Nations in Rome (FAO Bulletin 40). The Chinese regard biogas production as especially attractive because in addition to the fuel value of the biogas, the manure (sludge) is found to be richer than manure when composted.

The FAO report states that the Chinese people regard a pig as a "costless fertilizer factory moving on hooves." In a single year, a pig generates sufficient manure to supply fertilizer to increase grain output by 100 to 150 kilograms. Therefore, the fertilizer value of the yearly output of manure from 20 to 30 swine would be equal to that of one ton of ammonium sulfate.

The totals of such "costless fertilizer factories"—and their output—in China are both astronomical and highly significant to agricultural output. An insight into the amount of manure generated annually can be gained by the knowledge that in 1976 the Chinese pig population amounted to 238 million, each yielding about 300 kilograms of manure per year. The population of other livestock (cattle, water buffalos, donkeys, mules, and camels) was about 98 million head in 1976, and the number of sheep and goats amounted to 135 million.

While biogasification has chiefly been regarded as a promising method for developing countries, the more industrialized areas are now looking at the process more closely. In the United States, for example, the Pacific Gas and Electric Company and the Southern California Gas Company are building a manure-to-methane test facility at a cattle feedlot. Besides methane recovery, the companies plan to utilize the end product as a high-protein cattle feed.

Bio-Gas of Colorado, Inc., designed, built, and operates the facility, which will convert one ton of manure from 75 to 100 head of cattle daily to 7,000 cubic feet of natural gas. The utility companies envision expanding the demonstration project into commercial-size plants capable of processing manure from 50,000 to 400,000 head of cattle. Preliminary investigations have shown that approximately 30 million cubic feet of methane daily can potentially be produced from feedlot waste throughout California.

In Golden, Colorado, the Coors Brewery recovers valuable nutrients in its wastes for use as animal feed.

8

Putting Industrial Wastes to Use

The Westvaco Corporation of Luke, Maryland, received a 1977 environmental award from the American Paper Institute for making "synthetic topsoil" from its solid-waste by-product of the paper-making process. The material was used to reclaim abandoned coal strip-mines in western Maryland.

In Golden, Colorado, the Coors Brewery uses a Carver-Greenfield drying process to recover the high amounts of crude protein and vitamin B-12 in its brewery wastes for subsequent use as animal feed supplement. Coors also operates a cash-for-cans aluminum-recycling project in the western states in which its beer is marketed. In the first six months of 1978, Coors collected 36,792,130 pounds of aluminum.

The Reynolds Aluminum Recycling Company, a subsidiary of Reynolds Metals Company, collected a record-breaking 70 million pounds of aluminum through its consumer recycling program in the first half of 1978. Reynolds pays 17 cents per pound for aluminum beverage cans and other household aluminum items.

A subsidiary of the Campbell Soup Company, Technological

Resources, has been involved in research, design, installation, and the operation of land-treatment systems for food-plant wastewater for more than 20 years. Land-treatment systems can recycle nutrients in wastes from food-processing plants—bakeries, poultry processing, mushroom growing, vegetable processing, and frozen food.

For years, a group known as the Chemurgic Council monitored new uses for industrial wastes, and there are many indeed. Chemurgy is the branch of applied chemistry that deals with the utilization of organic raw materials, especially from farm products.

Louisiana State University operated a pilot plant which fermented sugar cane bagasse into edible single-cell protein with the texture of rough flour at a cost competitive with soybean flour or cornmeal.

The Research Center of the Bureau of Mines has used fly ash, a by-product of electric generating plants, as a partial substitute for cement in a sidewalk in Morgantown, West Virginia.

Kiln dust from the Hercules Cement Company was found to compare favorably with hydrated lime for vacuum filter processing of sewage sludge.

Owens-Illinois has used ground glass from disposable bottles as the aggregate material in paving a parking area and approach roads at its technical center in Toledo.

As it becomes apparent that state and federal regulations will compel industries to keep more of their wastes out of the public sewer system, air currents, and walkways, many companies are developing "closed-loop" systems for recovering those materials.

The volume and variety of industrial wastes offer tremendous potential for the creation of valuable materials. The following overview of what they are and some indications of ways to use them is based on Environmental Protection Agency estimates of industrial-sector sludges and reports published in the magazine *Compost Science/Land Utilization*.

The Food Industry

The food industry generates an estimated 650,000 tons of sludge per year. Of this amount, meat products account for 500,000 tons per year; dairy products, 100,000 tons per year; and canned and frozen foods, 50,000 tons per year.

Since the raw materials are from plants and animals, they are mainly organic, and landspreading or irrigating are the preferred methods of disposal. A recent survey indicated that 41 percent of the vegetable-processing plants and 37 percent of the fruit-processing plants used land disposal. An application rate of 10 to 20 tons per acre per year for solid waste was reported.

The following descriptions of several food industry wastes indicate their potential agricultural uses.

Apple Pomace: Apple pomace decays readily if mixed with material that provides for proper aeration. Its value in the wet state is not high, since the nitrogen content is only 0.2 percent. But ash content had over 3 percent phosphoric acid. The potash content is much higher, amounting to about 12 percent of the ash.

Brewery Wastes: Spent hops is the residue after hops have been extracted with water in the brewery. On a dry basis, the nitrogen ranges from 2.5 to 3.5 percent and the phosphoric acid about 1 percent.

The Sapporo Breweries Ltd., one of the big three beer makers in Japan, is reported to be composting its brewery wastes with equipment developed by Shinko Seisakusho Ltd., a company that specializes in manufacturing bottling machinery. Both capital and operating costs are claimed to be one-fourth those for conventional drying. Sapporo has installed the first plant at its Northern Kanto Brewery north of Tokyo, and plans to use the process in its eight other plants.

The process is designed to treat sludge produced from the brewery's wastewater treatment in the following way. First, about

30 percent (by weight) of waste malt, sawdust, and chaff are added to sludge, which is about 85 percent water. The mixture is then placed in a fermentation tank. The system includes seven tanks, and the contents of each are transferred to another tank daily.

The first Sapporo compost plant has a daily capacity of six tons. The finished material is sold to a local agricultural cooperative as well as to individual farmers.

Cannery and Dairy Wastes: More and more successful experiments are being conducted with spray irrigation, where vegetable canners and others are pumping waste products back to the land through sprinkler irrigation systems. Ohio State University reports that cannery wastes handled this way add to the organic matter of the soil, increase crop yields, and are free of undesirable odors.

Whey: A recent report by the University of Wisconsin described the possibilities of using excess whey as a soil builder: three tons of cheese whey contain about as much plant food as a ton of manure. Soil scientists studying the fertilizing value of whey believe this cheese industry by-product has promise as a fertilizer in areas near cheese plants. Four years of study indicate that whey applications of 20 to 50 tons per acre stimulate grass growth.

Tomato Pulp: During tomato processing, large quantities of tomato pulp or waste are generated. The material has value as a feed for livestock, but to be consistently used it needs to be treated and stored for later use. Researchers at Penn State University tested ensiling, and found that mixing the pulp with corn produced a desirable silage feed for cattle.

The use of food wastes for increasing crop production is especially important in many developing countries. Following a recent mission for the Food and Agriculture Organization of the United Nations, Dr. Cord Tietjen noted how a substance as common as coir dust (a residue of coconut husk manufacturing) could be used in the Philippines to suppress weeds and conserve moisture in plant rows. The same observation applied to rice hulls, bagasse, and cane trash.

In areas like Taiwan, western Malaysia, Israel, Yugoslavia, and Hungary, organic wastes are used to grow fish, a process which not only makes efficient use of wastes but also helps to purify the water. In the United States, aquaculture researchers at the Parr Fisheries in Kinmundy, Illinois, have successfully raised Chinese carp on hog manure.

The Textile Industry

The textile industry generates an estimated 300,000 tons per year of sludge, and a significant portion of this solid waste is organic. Although the dyes are complex organics, they should not occur in concentrations that are harmful. Sludges will result from detergents, sizing, and other chemicals, but these ingredients are not considered dangerous per se, as they are common components in municipal sewage.

The textile sludges can be divided into those derived from natural products such as cotton and those derived from synthetic fibers such as polyester. The fate and effects of the degradation products of cotton are likely to be known; of synthetic fibers, however, they are largely unknown.

Waste production in the textile industry includes organic and inorganic wet chemicals and purely dry products. There are four types of textile products—animal, vegetable, regenerated, and synthetic.

Some examples of textile wastes and their uses are:

Cotton Gin Waste: The cotton seed burrs are a source of potash. The fine waste and the more voluminous amounts of wastes containing cotton fiber are, as a rule, rich in nitrogen, because seed parts and lint are contained in them. When piled up in the open, this

This shredder-baler at a New Jersey paper-dealer plant bundles waste cartons at 10 tons per hour. The unit operates continuously for 10 hours per day, six days per week.

material will decay in a few months under southern conditions into a rich and valuable compost.

Wool Wastes (or shoddy): Shoddy has been used by British farmers living in the vicinity of wool textile mills since the Industrial Revolution in the early 19th century. Its fertilizing value lies entirely in its organic and nitrogen content.

The Pulp and Paper Industry

The pulp industry generates an estimated 2 million tons per year of sludge. These wastes are highly carbonaceous, resulting from undergraded cellulose fibers and biomass grown from the liquors of chemical solvents and dissolved liquor. Although technically not a food-chain product, the raw material is derived from plant life. Landspreading has been practiced in this industry for at least 20 years.

An estimated 200,000 tons of sludge per year is generated by the paper industry, with cellulose the major organic constituent of this sludge. Also resulting from paper-making are inorganic fillers, dyes, and sizing.

The most common types of paper produced are kraft, sulfite, neutral sulfite, semichemical, and groundwood. Some textile fibers are grown for use in specialty papers; these include flax, cotton, and jute.

Paper wastes exert a high biochemical oxygen-demand load because they contain compounds such as sugar, resins, tannins, and lignins. Inorganic compounds which are in a reduced state, such as sulfite, also utilize oxygen as they oxidize after being discharged.

Waste Bark: The millions of tons of waste bark generated in North America has considerable value as a soil conditioner. Research in Belgium has shown the value of composting to reduce the carbon/nitrogen ratio and to decompose the phytotoxins.

The Pharmaceuticals Industry

An estimated 200,000 tons of pharmaceutical sludges are generated per year. Solvents and hazardous biological and mineral wastes are incinerated or otherwise handled separately. The remaining 80,000 tons per year are organic and considered nonhazardous.

"Composting has been the best and most practical method of treatment, disposal, and utilization of pharmaceutical wastes," according to Anthony J. Gabaccia, former head of the Industrial Waste Department of Lederle Laboratories in Pearl River, New York.

Six to ten tons of organic sludges accumulated daily at the Pearl River plant, coming from fermentation of antibiotics, extraction of pharmaceuticals from animal livers, the animal stables, and the sanitary sewage from 4,000 employees. Composting converted this material to a granular, free-flowing, dark-brown material, with a slight humus odor, which is used on Lederle's grounds, by the nearby communities, or sold through a local dealer mainly for lawn treatment and soil conditioning.

The Leather Industry (Tanneries)

The leather industry generates about 100,000 tons of sludge per year. Sodium chloride salt is washed out of the cured hides, and lime and other alkalies are used to dehair and prepare hides for tanning and dying. Although tanning is organic, chrome tanning agents are commonly used. In some cases, chrome recovery may be practiced; when it is not, as much as 1 percent of the dry weight of the sludge may be chromium, thereby posing potential environmental problems.

Among waste materials in this group, the most valuable are those of tanneries such as the cuttings of hides and skins because of the high content of organically bound nitrogen. The N content of tanned hides, for instance, is 6–10 percent; that of raw hides, 12–13 percent. Such waste is used in France where the material is either composted or treated with acid and alkaline aqueous solutions in a process to make organic fertilizer.

Feedlots

Feedlots generate an estimated 50 million tons of manure per year. Although collected directly rather than as a sludge from a unit process, manures can be likened to domestic primary-sewage sludge. Landspreading has been the preferred, time-honored disposal method, since manure is used extensively as a soil conditioner and has a recognized fertilizer value. Composting trials and commercial developments have proven the value of composting prior to marketing.

The Petroleum Industry

An estimated 850,000 tons of petroleum residuals are produced per year. Solid wastes resulting from petroleum production include spent lime from boiler feed-water tanks, plus various organic sludges. About 10 percent of the residue is presently treated, while the rest is landfilled and lagooned. One treatment involves land application for aerobic biological oxidation of organic or oily wastes and for photochemical oxidation of tetraethyl lead wastes. Several oil companies have conducted composting trials.

The Metals Industry

Using ferrous scraps for steelmaking leads to a 74-percent saving in energy, 86 percent lower pollution, 76 percent less water pollution, a 90-percent saving in virgin materials, and 97 percent fewer mining wastes. The figures come from the Institute of Scrap Iron and Steel, which also points out that the energy savings can be interpreted as saving the equivalent of 140,000 gallons of gasoline for every 1,000 tons of steel manufactured from ferrous scrap.

The use of secondary copper conserves nearly 90 percent of the energy required when virgin ore is utilized. With titanium, the energy reduction is 70 percent.

While some 5 billion cans were recycled in 1977, the total is equal to only 5 percent of the steel cans manufactured domestically each year.

A few years ago, Dr. Monroe S. Wechsler and his fellow metallurgists at the University of Iowa tackled the problem of junked cars—and they represent a huge potential for recycling. According to figures compiled by Anthony Wolff (cited in *Science Digest*), 15 percent of the 6 to 8 million cars junked in the U.S. annually are never reprocessed. They rust away in a variety of places all over the country, representing millions of tons of resource if they were to be used.

Dr. Wechsler and his colleagues determined that a major deterrent to recycling was caused by nonferrous "contaminants," small amounts of copper, nickel, chromium, etc. The steel industry wants only limited amounts of such "contaminated" steel. After experimenting with a vacuum-melting process that bombarded the scrap with electrons, the researchers then devised a procedure called electroslag remelting. "In these experiments," wrote Wolff, "electricity flows directly through the scrap 'compact' to the mold, passing through a layer of powdered vitreous material, called slag, in between." As the slag melts, impurities are separated, leaving pure iron. Now Dr. Wechsler sees the big challenge to be in the commercial arena where policies are set for the big steel companies, as his research shows that the "junk" in automobiles can be recycled.

"In current terminology," Dr. Wechsler commented in the *Science Digest* report, "auto scrap has been treated as an economic externality. But, as populations grow and the store of resources dwindles on our finite world, such externalities will become of central importance."

The Rubber Industry

A tiny fraction of the 2 billion old tires that have been discarded recently wind up as swings for children when they are tied by rope to an overhanging tree branch. Another small fraction is used for bumpers on tow trucks, ferryboats, and barges. Give or take a few, that probably still leaves something like 1.99 billion to deal with— while many children and ferryboat captains do their thing.

Industries do some recycling when old tires are used as a catalyst in the vulcanizing process of manufacturing new tires. More aggressive use may take place if a process for applying reclaimed rubber to hot asphalt mix catches on. The mixture creates an improved surface for paving, and was developed by the U.S. Rubber Reclaiming Co. of Vicksburg, Mississippi.

Tire manufacturers are also researching new uses for old tires. Firestone developed a destructive distillation process in which shredded tires are fed into a reactor where temperatures range from 500° to 900°C. Firestone hopes to recover carbon black and oils for reuse in rubber manufacture. Other potential uses for old tires include making artificial fishing reefs. B. F. Goodrich, for example, has calculated that some 1½ billion tires could be used to attract fish off Montauk Point, Long Island, New York, and off the Miami, Florida, coast. To construct reefs, eight tires are connected with steel rods, mounted on a concrete base, and then sunk. Other uses being tested are making carbon black, and using tires as fuel to generate steam.

Industrial Waste Information Exchange*

As industrial waste disposal and treatment costs increase, so will the desire and interest of the manufacturing sector in reducing waste generation and finding alternative disposal systems. One alternative disposal method which is rapidly gaining popularity, from both the private sector and government, is the Industrial Waste Exchange.

Waste Exchange programs are simple in design: the goal is to connect waste generators with potential waste users. Solid waste volumes will decrease by finding a suitable reuse value, thereby lowering disposal and treatment costs for the generator and lowering the cost of raw materials for the potential user.

The Waste Exchange idea began in the Netherlands in 1972 and quickly spread to several other European countries. The first American exchange was the St. Louis Industrial Waste Exchange, which dates from January 1976. Since that time, 22 other American exchange programs have started, supported by either state or local governments, or by private industry associations. Most programs are nonprofit, although five are for profit. The best sponsor for an exchange program is either a state government (as in Oregon), or a large industry association (as in Georgia, where the sponsor is the Georgia Business and Industry Association). The reasons for this are quite obvious: (1) industry participation, support, and confidence are necessary for a successful exchange, and (2) exchange operations usually do not have a financial base of support other than the state or local government, or an industry or trade association.

Waste Exchange programs are either passive or active in their approach to the problem and in the services they offer. In the United States, exchanges range from strictly passive (Iowa), to passive with

*The following was written by Kevin Mulligan, a principal in Resource Conservation Consultants of Portland, Oregon. Mr. Mulligan was an organizer of the Portland Recycling Team, one of the largest full-time recyclers in the U.S., and has extensive experience in recycling and waste reduction programs in the Northwest.

an active solicitation (Oregon and Minnesota), to active material exchanges (the Natural Resources Recycling Exchange in Boston). A passive exchange usually deals only in the exchange of information, while an active exchange works like a materials broker, actually buying, treating, processing, storing, and reselling the materials. The majority of exchange programs in the United States are passive. Most exchange programs are also free, although some do charge a small subscription fee for the listings bulletin.

The basic service of the Oregon Industrial Waste Information Exchange (sponsored by the Oregon Department of Energy) is typical of most American exchanges. Listings of available wastes and requests for waste materials wanted arrive at the exchange office on a regular basis. Once every other month the exchange issues a bulletin to industries throughout the state which lists these waste materials. Parties who are interested in these wastes contact the exchange office, which then arranges for the waste generator and the potential user to get together for the purpose of a transfer. The exchange office does not place a value on these waste materials, nor does it participate in any of the negotiations. However, the Oregon exchange office does offer research services that will attempt to analyze the composition of a waste and will attempt to solicit potential users to help facilitate a transfer.

The economic factors affecting a successful transfer are quite simple: the party interested in the waste must find the cost of obtaining the waste material (purchase price, transportation, processing, and treatment) to be less expensive than the cost of raw materials or products which are currently being used. For the party interested in disposing of the waste, the primary concern is to reduce its disposal cost by giving the waste materials away, or at least paying less for a transfer than the present cost of treatment and disposal. Of course, in some cases the party disposing of the waste material will want to receive payment for it if it has a known value. This will call for more involved negotiations than usual.

Another important factor in a successful transfer is the problem of corporate confidentiality. Manufacturers naturally want to protect their industrial secrets and processing techniques from their competitors. Therefore, it is essential that listings not identify the waste generator or the party interested in obtaining the waste. Because of this, all waste exchanges in the United States list materials available and materials wanted by a code number known only to them, thus protecting the anonymity of the parties involved.

Because of a lack of sufficient studies on the amount of waste materials generated, and the types of wastes available and potentially useful, it is difficult to gauge the maximum transfer potential for waste materials through the exchange mechanism. However, the U.S. Environmental Protection Agency, in a study conducted by the Arthur D. Little Company, estimates that there are 206 million metric tons of industrial waste generated per year (wet basis). Out of this, it is estimated that about 6 million metric tons per year, or about 3 percent, have a transfer or reuse value.

However, within certain manufacturing fields, the potential transfer for selected types of wastes is much higher. For instance, the EPA has estimated that the transfer possibilities may be as high as 95 percent in pharmaceuticals, 66 percent in petroleum refining, and 40 percent in paints and allied products. Other wastes which are considered to have high transfer potential include: alkalies, solvents, organic chemicals, oils, combustibles, catalysts, and metals.

One thing to bear in mind concerning successful transfers is that the quantity of an available waste material will often have a great bearing on the transfer potential. While there are some transfer possibilities for small amounts of wastes, or for one-time-only wastes, most potential users demand large amounts that are available on a regular basis.

In addition to the difficulty in knowing how many wastes, and what types, have a potential reuse value, there appears to be no standard system to evaluate successful transfers. Most exchanges in the United States do not appear to place an emphasis on recording successful transfers, and of those that do, most depend on voluntary replies from the parties involved and this information is often incomplete and inaccurate.

Evidence from the European exchange experience suggests that approximately 10 percent of those materials listed are actually transferred. However, in some cases, and with specific types of wastes, this figure has been as high as 30 percent. Although most American exchanges are too new to gauge the results of transfer listings effectively, the evidence available so far suggests that 10 percent might be a reasonable figure to expect in most areas of the United States. Of course the transfer potential will be higher in areas of high industrialization such as New Jersey, Illinois, and Ohio.

While there are not yet enough exchange programs, or studies of the programs that do exist, to fully judge the potential effects of this type of approach to industrial waste disposal and management, we can look at some obvious beneficial results:

1. Any program which can control the flow of hazardous wastes, which represents 10–15 percent of all industrial wastes, from generation to disposal will directly and immediately benefit health and environmental quality.
2. Municipal sludge utilization and its land application capabilities will be significantly enhanced by the removal of many industrial by-products and metals before the sludge is subjected to a treatment process.
3. Industrial business managers will hopefully look to new and alternate means of disposal and materials reuse if they have successful results with transferring wastes through an exchange program.
4. A mechanism will be available to states to enable them to comply with the new disposal regulations and standards as they develop.

5. In some industrial sectors, significant economic benefits will be realized in the cost and consumption of raw materials and resources, and in waste-disposal costs.

A list of waste exchanges in the United States appears below.

Waste Exchanges in the U.S.

American Chemical Exchange
4849 Golf Road
Skokie, IL
(312) 677-2800   Robert Anderson

Calspan Industrial Waste Exchange
Sponsor: Calspan Corp.
P.O. Box 235
Buffalo, NY 14221
(716) 632-7500 X547
For Profit

Chemical Recycle Information
Sponsor: Houston Chamber of Commerce
1100 Milam Bldg.
Houston, TX 77002
(713) 651-1313   Jack Westney

Enkarn Research Corp.
(Industrial Materials Bulletin)
P.O. Box 590
Albany, NY 12201
(518) 436-9684   Ken Carney

Environmental Clearinghouse Exchange
Environmental Clearinghouse Org., Inc.
3426 Maple Lane
Hazel Crest, IL 60429
(312) 335-0754   Bill Petrich
For Profit

Georgia Waste Exchange
Sponsor: Georgia Business & Industry Assn.
181 Washington St., SW
Atlanta, GA 30303
(404) 659-4444   Steve McWilliams

Information Center for Waste Exchange
Sponsor: Western Environmental Trade Assn.-WA
314 Park Place Bldg.
Seattle, WA 98101
(206) 623-5235   Judy Henry

Iowa Industrial Waste Information
Exchange
Center for Industrial Research &
Service
201 Building E, Iowa State
University
·Ames, IA 50011
(515) 294-4320
Edward O. Sealine   W.A. Kluckman

Minnesota Assn of Commerce &
Industry
(Control Data Corp.)
200 Hanover Bldg., 480 Cedar St.
St. Paul, MN 55101
(612) 227-9591   James T. Shields

The Natural Resource Recycling
Exchange
286 Congress St.
Boston, MA 02210
(617) 482-2727   Howell Hurst
For Profit

Oregon Industrial Waste Information
Exchange
1615 NW 23rd, Suite One
Portland, OR 97210
(503) 227-1319   Jerry Powell

St. Louis Industrial Waste Exchange
10 Broadway
St. Louis, MO 63102
(314) 231-5555   Roland Marquart

Tennessee Waste Swap
Sponsor: Division of Solid Waste
Mgmt.
TN Dept. of Public Health
320 Capitol Hill Bldg.
Nashville, TN 37219
(615) 741-3424

Waste
152 Utah Ave. "F"
South San Francisco, CA 94080
(415) 871-1711   John T. Nightingale
For Profit

Zero Waste System, Inc.
2928 Poplar St.
Oakland, CA 94608
(415) 893-8257   Paul Palmer
For Profit

California Waste Exchange
California State Health Dept.
Vector & Waste Mgmt.
2151 Berkeley Way
Berkeley, CA 94704
(415) 843-7900 X434

Industrial Waste Clearinghouse
Environmental Quality Control, Inc.
1220 Waterway Blvd.
Indianapolis, IN 46202
(317) 634-2142   Noble L. Beck

Industrial Waste Information
Exchange
Sponsor: Columbus Industrial Assn.
1515 W. Lane Ave.
Columbus, OH 43221
(614) 486-6741

Industrial Waste Information
Exchange
Sponsor: New Jersey Chamber of
Commerce
5 Commerce Street
Newark, NJ 70102
(201) 623-7070

Mecklenburg County
Engineering Dept.
1501 I-85 North
Charlotte, NC 28216
(704) 374-2770

Union Carbide
Surplus Products Group
Investment Recovery Dept.
270 Park Ave.
New York, NY 10017
(212) 551-2345
For Profit

Syracuse Waste Exchange
Sponsor: Allied Chemical
P.O. Box 6
Solvay, NY 13209
(315) 487-4198

9

The Nation's Recycling "Industrial Complex"

Recycling involves one of the most dynamic and technically complex industries in the nation, explains a public relations message from the National Association of Recycling Industries (NARI). "The recycling industry has fully emerged from what was once rudimentary scrap collection to what is today one of the most sophisticated and vitally important industries in the United States," claims the association's executive vice-president, M. J. Mighdoll.

Secondary-materials dealers, scrap dealers, junk dealers, leading steel and packaging corporations, and a host of others are represented by national organizations in solid-waste management/resource recovery. Here are some of the prominent ones:

> Aluminum Association
> American Iron and Steel Institute
> American Paper Institute
> Beverage Industry Recycling Program
> Can Manufacturers Institute, Inc.
> Glass Packaging Institute

Institute of Scrap Iron and Steel
National Association of Recycling Industries
National Center for Resource Recovery, Inc.
National Solid Waste Management Association
Packaging Institute, U.S.A.
Paperboard Packaging Council
Rubber Manufacturers Association
Society of the Plastics Industry, Inc.
U.S. Brewers Association

The above list indicates the scope of interest in materials to be recycled, motivations, public relations, and so forth. The data supplied by many of the above organizations can give one the impression that all is well in the resource-recovery world. In a handsome NARI brochure, "Recycling Responds," we are informed that "recycled materials are found in virtually everything we use—from our automobiles to the paper we write on." The crunch issue, of course, is what percentage of recycled materials are used. The following statistics appear in the NARI report:

About 45 to 50 million tons of ferrous scrap are recovered annually. Some 12 million tons of paper and close to 3 billion pounds of textiles are recycled each year, along with thousands of tons of rubber (4 percent of the total). Over 40 percent of the nation's copper comes from the recycling process, almost half of its lead, 25 percent of its aluminum, 14 percent of the zinc, and about 20 percent of the paper and paperboard.

A regional study of recycling potential from municipal wastes in the San Francisco Bay Area was commissioned in 1976 by the California Solid Waste Management Board. Estimating that some 9

The wide range of scrap metals that accumulates at a dealer's "junkyard" reflects both the amount and variety of material that can be reused through recycling programs.

million tons of solid wastes will be generated by 1980 in that area, the researchers evaluated the following recovery considerations:

FIBER

Mixed wastepaper composes approximately 40–50 percent of the residential/commercial solid-waste stream and could be absorbed by direct users (manufacturers of linerboard and roofing felt) and by the paper broker. Indications are that the San Francisco Bay Area paper stock companies could absorb 100 to 200 tons per day of mixed waste paper at $5 to $10 per ton.

FERROUS

Sufficient markets (steel remelt, copper precipitation, detinners, and scrap dealers) are available to absorb all the ferrous material that could be recovered in the Bay Area. Prices in the range of $25 to $40 per ton can be obtained. The prices depend on the quality of the end product.

ALUMINUM

There are sufficient markets available to absorb all the aluminum potentially recoverable from the waste stream provided that the specifications can be met. However, the technology for large-scale aluminum recovery remains untested, and therefore the quality of the end product cannot be determined at this time. Prices for aluminum range from $200 to $500 per ton.

GLASS

There are several glass manufacturers around the Bay Area which could individually accept on the order of 200 tons per day of clean, color-sorted glass cullet at a price of $20 per ton. Unfortunately, the state of the art in glass recovery has not developed to the

Record-breaking amounts of aluminum cans have been collected through programs like that run by Reynolds Aluminum Recycling Company, which pays 17 cents per pound.

stage where a recovered glass cullet fraction can economically meet the rigid specifications set by the glass manufacturers.

ASPHALT

With the rising price of petroleum pushing the cost of asphalt to as much as $16 a ton, the technology to strip off old asphalt, melt it down, and recondition it is developing beyond the experimental stage. According to a recent article in the *Wall Street Journal*, some states have been recognizing savings on the average of 20–30 percent.

Iowa, Texas, Kansas, California, Utah, Oregon, Minnesota, and Arizona all have recycling programs. In Iowa, the Department of Transportation reports that about 5 percent of the state's paving will be done with recycled asphalt this year. This total, they say, may eventually rise to 30 percent. A spokesman from Iowa said that they not only use recycled asphalt because it costs less, but also because the quality is a little better than new asphalt.

One big problem, however, according to the *Wall Street Journal*, is that recycling asphalt generates huge amounts of air pollution. But the state of Minnesota reports that a cleaner process has been developed.

COMPOST

Markets for two types of compost were investigated. One type was made from somewhat segregated plant debris and manures, while the other was made from the organic fraction of solid wastes and sludge. Only the first type (that produced from plant debris) showed limited marketability in the Bay Area.

ENERGY

The potential for utilizing energy derived from refuse was

considered in terms of solid, liquid, and gaseous forms. A survey of the largest gas users in the Bay Area was conducted. Solid fuel (RDF) was considered as light fraction in both fluff and densified form. Constraints on using solid fuels stem from the fact that most boilers in the Bay Area do not have ash removal equipment. Under certain conditions, suitable markets exist for using this material in conjunction with conventional fossil fuels provided that certain incentives are granted to prospective users.

━━━━━━━━━━━━━━━━━━━━━━━━━━━━━━━━

Turning Trash into Cash is the title of a United States Steel pamphlet designed to increase those percentages, stressing that "we're creating more waste than we can deal with efficiently." The only permanent, practical solution, says USS, is communitywide "resource recovery."

Ames, Iowa (population 45,000), is described as one of America's most successful models for resource recovery. In 1977, the city processed more than 48,000 tons of waste; 80–85 percent was recovered in the form of combustible fuel and 6.2 percent as magnetically separated ferrous metals. The dollar value of the fuel was calculated at about $350,000, and the ferrous metal value exceeded $100,000. It has been estimated that when the system is able to recover 60,000 tons per year, the program will cost less than many landfills in the state. However, present costs are more than 10 times the original estimates, running in excess of $15 per ton as opposed to $1.20 per ton.

The general concept is that about 75 percent of all municipal waste can be converted into some form of energy, usually by being burned as a supplementary fuel. The 5–7 percent of ferrous metals, aluminum, copper, and brass can be sorted out mechanically for salvage.

Pilot and full-scale projects have begun—some are struggling along at only fractions of original recovery rates—in such places as

San Francisco, Milwaukee, New Orleans, Saugus, Massachusetts, and Hempstead, New York. The Hempstead facility is designed to be a 2,000-ton-per-day unit which will yield 15 percent of the community's residential electricity load. The design is a scaled-up version of the Black Clawson plant in Franklin, Ohio, where garbage is fed into "hydrapulpers" and material is salvaged. Problems have plagued such plants to date, including periodic explosions when garbage is shredded.

Nevertheless, a number of resource-recovery plants (many feature refuse-derived fuel) are in the design stage—Akron, Ohio (900 tons per day); Bridgeport, Connecticut (1,650 tpd); Monroe County, New York (1,800 tpd); Detroit (2,700 tpd); Hackensack, New Jersey (1,800 tpd). At Pompano Beach, Florida, a 45–90 tpd anaerobic digester has been operating as a demonstration facility.

Refuse-derived fuel (RDF) presents difficulties for efficient use since it is more difficult to store and retrieve than conventional fuels, being a heterogeneous mixture of unpredictable content. According to a paper presented at the American Society of Mechanical Engineers' 1978 Conference by Henry Lisiecki, "the formation of self-supporting masses of material that will not move as planned through the storage system plague many RDF systems. Fires, though less common, are a special impediment to successful storage of large quantities of RDF in single structures."

The disadvantages of RDF and other basic concepts of large-scale resource-recovery systems are rarely mentioned in the drive to convert the multibillion-dollar dumping industry into a multibillion-dollar resource-recovery industrial complex. The process, as envisioned by major industry developers, begins with the consumer piling up as much (or more) garbage and trash as now. Collection trucks would no longer deliver their loads to a landfill or dump, however. Instead, the trucks would deposit wastes onto a large conveyor for delivery into a shredder. Then the material would be magnetically separated or air classified, thereby separating lighter particles (paper, plastics, etc.) from metal and glass.

Depending on the volume of wastes processed, different routes would be established. Smaller communities could contract with secondary-materials dealers to process materials further; larger cities might be advised to set up a magnetic retrieval system for ferrous metals, and to sort out glass, aluminum, and other nonferrous metals. And then the final residue has potential for fuel— or, though few of the major industry publications ever mention it, the ground residue would be most suitable for composting.

Potential vs. Actual Markets

As everyone who has ever participated in community recycling drives has discovered, there are wide swings in the market prices for recycled materials. The frustration of sorting, collecting, and storing wastepaper—and then being forced to dump it—has been experienced by many citizen recyclers.

Scrap dealers can only recycle what there is a market demand for. And real problems occur when the demand tapers or disappears entirely. The National Association of Recycling Industries places great emphasis on industrial consumers as the key to fulfilling the potential. "It must be remembered that without sustained and expanded industrial market demand for recovered raw materials, the collection process alone can become counterproductive to recycling efforts," the NARI warns.

Industrial consumers include the refineries that convert scrap into new, refined copper, aluminum smelters that produce ingots for castings and other fabricated products. They are the steel mills that absorb huge tonnages of scrap iron and steel, brass mills and ingot manufacturers, smelters of lead and zinc, paper mills and paperboard manufacturers, textile product and rubber manufacturers, and hundreds of other industries that use recycled raw materials in their daily operations.

Thus the industrial complex for resource recovery includes both the consumer segment and the manufacturing segment.

In an attempt to recover more of the 100 million tons of potential value in their annual wastes, European countries are focusing on some steps to stabilize supply in the secondary-materials market. These include stockpiling secondary materials during times of low demand and using long-term contracts when both the reclaimer and user agree on a price and organize their operations over a fixed period during which little or no account is taken of the prevailing market prices.

According to a report on "Resource Recovery in Europe," published by the National Center for Resource Recovery, Inc., the Norwegian Department of Environmental Protection provides low-interest loans to finance the paper industry's stockpiling operations. In Germany, the idea of standard contract conditions for the supply of secondary materials by local authorities is being examined.

A regulation that requires wastepaper to be collected separately is an approach that has been adopted in Sweden. By 1980, most Swedish residents will be required by law to separate wastepaper in homes, shops, and offices. Explains the NCRR report: "The measure was taken because industrialists within the paper industry in Sweden were prepared to make the investment in increased wastepaper processing plants but they laid down as a condition of such expansion that the supply of wastepaper should be guaranteed. As an immediate result, large stocks of wastepaper have been built up; however, industry has agreed to increase de-inking capacity so that the wastepaper can be used for a wider range of products."

The Case Against High-Technology Recycling

In the words of Neil Seldman of Washington's Institute for

Wide swings in market prices for recycled materials often frustrate recycling projects. The frustration of sorting, collecting, and storing paper—and then being forced to dump it—has been experienced by many citizen recyclers.

Local Self-Reliance, a major national battle is under way over who should control the directions and profits from recycling the millions of tons of municipal garbage produced annually. The battle is between the large corporations which belong to the kinds of associations mentioned at the beginning of this chapter, and advocates of such approaches as low-technology, neighborhood recycling systems. In some cases, it's a matter of scale; in others, it relates to an emphasis on closing the wastes–land cycle; in still others, it relates to the fundamental issue of simpler living habits that use less resources.

Ten years ago, Athelstan Spilhaus, who at that time headed the National Academy of Science's committee reporting on waste management and control, cited the "second law of thermodynamics" that tells us that as a product moves through a series of changes, it loses some energy in each change. Thus, as garbage moves further along the waste stream from individual home to centralized recovery plant, the more new energy must be introduced and the greater the cost to all. "It must be cheaper in energy (and energy costs money) to collect waste at the source before it has undergone a long series of changes and dispersals," Spilhaus said.

Countering the public-relations material heralding the wonders of resource-recovery installations that create refuse-derived fuel, etc., Dr. Seldman points to their failures. "Mechanical separation, combustion, and air-pollution control equipment have failed to work in plants in St. Louis, Baltimore, and Nashville. The result has been higher costs, delays, and the need for even more sophisticated technology which planners hope will correct the problems." Some cities, he explains, have even been forced to sign contracts with penalty clauses if they enact legislation to reduce the flow of the waste stream to proposed plants. The more trash produced, in other words, the more profitable the recovery system.

Seldman notes that such requirements enforcing high volumes are by no means in the best interests of recycling strategies. If, for example, paper is burned in an RDF plant, it may be worth $5 to $8 per ton based on its BTU value. If recycled as fiber, it may be valued at $10 or more per ton.

As an alternative to the resource-recovery "behemoths," many people suggest such approaches as source separation, mandatory-deposit beverage legislation, and comprehensive collection and recycling systems.

Bio-Gas of Colorado, Inc., is a recently formed company which specializes in the design of methane-recovery systems. Lab director Susan Schellenbach stands on a pilot unit. *(photo by Clarence E. Bennett)*

10

New Jobs and Careers
in Recycling Wastes

As the emphasis increases on recovering resources currently discarded as wastes—such as recycling metals, generating fuel, and composting—so also does the need for trained personnel, new businesses, well-designed systems, and special equipment. To satisfy that need, a broad range of career and business opportunities is emerging.

For example, after seven years of operating a wide-based recycling business in Portland, Oregon, Jerry Powell and Kevin Mulligan formed Resource Conservation Consultants to advise private and public agencies. The consulting firm is doing work for Seattle and other cities looking to source-separation systems as a viable part of their solid-waste management plans. Comments Jerry Powell:

> Only a handful of towns collected recyclables in 1971; now more than 250 communities offer such a service. Private enterprise is increasing their investment in reclamation projects, as evidenced by aluminum recycling projects in Arizona and Weyerhauser's large office paper recovery system. In other words, there is a growing audience for recycling.

In the opinion of Joseph Duckett of the National Center for Resource Recovery concerning career opportunities in waste recycling, the demand seems to be greatest for engineers with actual manufacturing experience (i.e., "hands-on" experience) or scientists with backgrounds in materials science, combustion theory, or aerodynamics. Says Duckett:

> There is not now—and there may never be—large numbers of new jobs created by the waste recycling industry. Research efforts have been on a very modest scale (compared to the nuclear energy industry, for example). Also, the resource recovery systems tend to employ relatively few people (a large plant may have 50 employees). Still the field is growing and is in great need of good people.
>
> The best preparation for work in waste recycling would probably be a firm foundation in some field of engineering or science (e.g., mechanical or civil engineering, chemistry, physics) coupled with some topical courses in materials science and waste management and some experience (maybe even summer jobs) with processing and laboratory equipment.

Michael Porter received his Master of Science degree in agricultural economics in 1978 from Purdue University. As a research assistant to Dr. Joseph Donnermeyer, he surveyed Indiana farmers about their willingness to accept treated municipal sewage sludge on their land as a fertilizer and/or soil conditioner. He identified the key management-related factors and social/attitudinal variables influencing farmer acceptance of sludge and its market potential.

As recycling wastes becomes a more widely established business area, a large number of factors must be addressed. Porter honed in on such factors: level of acceptance, types of farmers most likely to accept treated sludge, what information sources are important in the adoption of the process, delivery arrangements, product forms, and pricing conditions. The study provided a base of information for use by policymakers, government administrators, municipal officials, and others concerned with planning and implementing recycling programs.

When he received his MS in September 1978, Porter's career interests led him to seek employment with a multidisciplinary consulting firm that would allow him to use his training to develop recycling systems in the areas of land application of sludge/wastewater, as well as to perform economic-feasibility studies, environmental-impact analyses, and marketing-research investigations.

Porter's interests and talents are ones being increasingly sought by many consulting engineering firms which serve as a support system for the recycling field. Cal Recovery Systems, Inc., in Richmond, California, led by Dr. Luis Diaz, offers expertise in equipment and systems for turning municipal and industrial waste into useful materials. Jon Dyer of Environmental Technology Consultants is specializing in land recycling programs, and the Energy Resource Company in Cambridge, Massachusetts, has assembled a capable team of specialists in agronomy, engineering, and marketing. In Ohio, Jim Perry has formed the S & L Fertilizer Company and markets sludge from Toledo to farmers. Some of the largest consulting firms in the country are developing expertise in land recycling programs; Camp Dresser & McKee, for example, now has a public participation staffperson in its New York office to address that aspect of recycling projects.

The legal aspects of recycling wastes and applying them to land, from the siting of resource-recovery facilities to the institutional arrangements for contracts, require a sophisticated knowledge of the law. Joseph M. Manko and Bruce S. Katcher, members of a Philadelphia law firm, are concentrating on the legal developments which can "help disengage the time bomb that solid waste has always presented to the future of our nation and its people."

Speaking of municipal wastes and wastewater, another exciting field that is opening up and is directly related to recycling is on-site utilization of household wastewater. More and more companies now manufacture and market aerobic systems that include compost toilets. So much progress has been made that a trade association has been formed, the Alternative Wastewater Management Association (P.O. Box 32240, Washington, D.C. 20007).

In addition to such firms as Clivus Multrum, Enviroscope, and others which offer compost toilet equipment, the related services and complimentary businesses are also evolving. David del Porto and his ECOS, Inc., in Boston serve an important educational and marketing function. Domestic Environmental Alternatives in Hathaway Pines, California, is a small firm formed to provide home-owners in Calaveras and Tuolumne counties with ways to conserve water and energy, and to improve upon individual on-site sewage disposal systems. "Periodically," explains DEA's Janet Skenfield, "we offer free seminars to the community on such subjects as water conservation, alternative sewage disposal and solar energy. ...We now have a retail store, and this has been a big help in reaching people. It gives us the space to display all the products we have, a place where people can come for information, etc."

Her husband Michael and his partner Tom Scheller trouble-shoot faulty systems, design new ones, and distribute plumbing products ranging from the standard water and wastewater fixtures to the alternative low-water and waterless units. Such units include low-flow showerheads, low-flush toilets, compost toilets, and washwater irrigation systems.

Blends of high technology and low technology are often vital to developing successful recycling systems, the ratios depending on the scale of the project and the amount of capital available. Converting wastes into a fuel, biogas, illustrates the wide latitude.

Wayne Turnacliff is project engineer for Bio-Gas of Colorado, Inc., a firm specializing in the design of methane-recovery systems, also known as biogasification. Bio-Gas of Colorado has built a test facility for the Pacific Gas and Electric Company and the Southern California Gas Company that converts manure to methane. One tone of manure from 75 to 100 head of cattle will yield 7,000 cubic feet of natural gas daily. The utility companies envision expanding the demonstration project into commercial-size plants capable of

Richard Tichenor of Kittery, Maine, designed this three-part container for recycled materials in the home. It's an example of the kinds of devices needed to be developed for the commercial marketplace.

processing manure from 50,000 to 400,000 head of cattle. Preliminary investigations have shown that approximately 30 million cubic feet of methane daily can potentially be produced from feedlot waste throughout California.

Biogasification is one more example of how economists, researchers, and corporate officials are taking a new look at systems which maximize food production while optimizing waste utilization.

Markets can be expected to open up for home separation containers, as mandatory source-separation recycling systems are established. A pilot-scale version has been designed by Richard Tichenor of Recycling and Conservation, Inc., of Kittery, Maine. The stackable containers are used by residents of Nottingham, New Hampshire.

New Horizons for Vermiculture

One of the most intriguing developments in recycling is concerned with the use of earthworms to turn organic wastes into useful products. Sherrel Hall has founded the Ecology International Corporation which specializes in vermiculture, publishes the *Vermiculture Journal*, and designs worm-harvesting equipment.

The Arete Vermicomp Corp., led by Paul France, is setting up projects in eastern cities, and working with such researchers as Dr. Roy Hartenstein of SUNY College of Forestry at Syracuse and Prof. Nellie Stark of the University of Montana. Developments in this fledgling industry were described at a 1978 National Science Foundation–sponsored conference entitled "Utilization of Soil Organisms in Sludge Management."

Left: Planet Earthworms Company was formed by the McNellys of Boulder, Colorado, to make potting soil from waste materials.

Wormglenn is the title of a project planned by Jim McNelly who is working with Northglenn, a city in the Denver, Colorado, area. The concept integrates earthworm production with treated wastes from a municipally run methane digester, community grass clippings and shredded newspapers. As envisioned by McNelly, the prototype system "will utilize the most advanced recycling technologies with a modest capital investment in order to demonstrate the cost effectiveness." Included are modern management methods for worm herding, cultivation, and harvesting of egg capsules; production of compost; and marketing as a soil conditioner in the Denver area. McNelly is particularly enthusiastic about the opportunities of mass producing earthworm eggs for use as a low-cost protein source as feed for livestock.

New jobs are opening up with manufacturers of shredding equipment, magnetic separators, air classifiers, and conveying equipment specifically manufactured for use in recycling projects. A great push is on now to bring commerce, technology, and environmental and societal interests more closely together under the banner of *appropriate technology*. Recycling is an integral part of that effort.

In her book *Creating Alternative Futures*, Hazel Henderson included these observations about economics and corporate development, and the vital role to be played by renewable-resource management:

> We must build a new productive system based on recycling and renewable materials and energy sources such as solar, wind, wave, and geothermal energy; methane conversion from sewage and wastes; tree farming as well as bioengineering methods of production; and recycling employing enzymes and microorganisms. The new economy of permanence will require much technological innovation. It affords tremendous opportunities for entrepreneurship and initiative.

11

Mandatory Deposit Legislation and Recycling*

Some 15 million people live in states which have mandatory beverage-deposit legislation. Those people are faring quite well. Throughout the nation, other states and municipalities are considering the enactment of similar legislation; in fact, the federal government is debating the passage of a nationwide law.

Oregon, Vermont, Maine, Michigan, Iowa, and Connecticut, as of midyear 1978, have some kind of mandatory-deposit legislation, the earliest ones enacted in Vermont and Oregon in 1972. These deposit laws basically require a deposit on all beer and soda containers, without prohibiting any particular type of container (besides flip-top cans). While the thrust of the legislation is to encourage use of refillable bottles, it does allow consumers the freedom to purchase other types of containers which, when returned, would be recycled.

Such laws, seemingly encouraging all that is good without hurting anyone, have roused all kinds of fury and emotional debate. Mandatory-deposit laws, as opposed to other recycling systems,

*This chapter was written by Nora Goldstein.

affect not only people's consumption patterns but also industrial production, marketing, and employment. Even though the final overall effects of the deposit bills are positive—saving energy and resources, creating jobs—this "simple" change in the American throwaway mentality has caused much controversy and opposition to this sort of legislation.

For example, shortly after the Vermont law went into effect, the "Steel Products News Bureau" issued a release saying that "Vermont's ban on nonreturnable containers has resulted in a net loss to Vermonters at the rate of $1.8 million annually. . . . A survey of 44 retail grocers along Vermont's borders indicates beer sales during September dropped by 49 percent. The decline was attributed directly to Vermont's bottling law."

Interestingly, James Jeffords, the state's representative in Congress, and Donald Webster, director of its Environmental Conservation Agency, wrote an account of Vermont's experience with beverage-container deposit legislation over a four-year period entitled "Vermont 5¢ Deposit." The report sets forth much data to document the positive effects of the legislation.

The Vermont deposit system works this way. A deposit of at least five cents is required on each beer and soda container sold in the state, and is refunded when the container is returned to the store. Stores are required to accept containers of the size and type they sell, but are allowed to limit hours of redemption and to refuse to accept dirty or damaged containers. The beverage distributors, who pick up the containers from the retailers, are required to reimburse retailers for their handling costs at a standard rate of 20 percent of the amount of the deposit. In other words, the grocer is paid a penny for each five-cent container or two cents for each ten-cent container. An amendment passed in 1977 bans nonrefillable bottles, cans with removable tabs, and nonbiodegradable plastic rings for six-packs.

The initial opposition from such groups as the Vermont Labor Council (AFL–CIO) and the Vermont League of Cities and Towns gradually faded, and the Vermont Retail Grocers Association estimates that 95 percent of its membership supports the legislation now. There is a consensus that at least the worst of the initial fears—fears suggested by out-of-state opponents—have simply not materialized.

On the other hand, the goals have largely been satisfied. The original objective of the deposit bill, litter reduction, has been achieved, as 95 percent of all beverage containers are returned to stores. (Oregon found a 72-percent reduction in litter for the first year and an 83-percent reduction for the second year.) Since passage of the law, the State Highway Department has reduced its employee man-hours for litter pickup by 56.6 percent. Notes Representative Jeffords: "Some Vermonters have commented that the law's impact goes well beyond the expected reduction in beverage container litter; that the symbolic step away from our 'throwaway society' has influenced the attitudes of Vermonters and visitors, who are now less inclined to discard any form of litter on the roadsides."

Another positive side effect of the mandatory-deposit legislation in both Vermont and Oregon has been the energy savings due to returnable and refillable beverage containers. In Oregon the State Department of Environmental Quality has computed that Oregon has a net savings of 1.4 trillion BTUs per year, enough to supply the heating needs of 50,000 Oregon residents. In Vermont, using the Federal Energy Administration's formula for computing energy impact, the Jeffords–Webster report calculates Vermont's energy savings at 708 billion BTUs per year, or enough fuel oil to provide for the home heating needs of 15,000 Vermonters.

As more states begin to pass mandatory-deposit laws, the legislation is attempting to deal with any negative effects caused by the law. Besides the reimbursement to the retailers or distributors for handling costs, the state of Connecticut includes a provision in its law which establishes an "employee dislocation allowance training fund," to be administered by the labor commissioner. The Pennsylvania Alliance for Returnables notes that "the dislocation allowance is intended to assist any employee who loses his or her job directly because of the provisions of this law. This allowance is set at 75% of the average weekly earnings of the dislocated employee and includes, but is not limited to, retraining and employment reassistance and educational training programs."

Comparing Alternative Waste-Recovery Systems

Major opponents of mandatory-deposit legislation usually support resource-recovery systems based on the present throwaway mentality. However, according to one estimate by a Washington, D.C., public-interest group, packaging beer and soft drinks in approximately 60 billion throwaway containers rather than in returnable bottles wastes more than 200 trillion BTUs of energy in a single year. That energy wastage is equivalent to 18.2 billion kilowatt-hours of electricity or 1.7 billion gallons of gasoline.

Dr. Priscilla Laws, a physicist at Dickinson College, has computed that almost 1 percent of the nation's energy is wasted in the production of throwaways. A group in Illinois (Housewives Interested in Pollution Solutions) calculated that consumers paid $1.5 billion more than the same beverages would cost in returnable bottles, and that taxpayers contributed at least another $350 million annually to dispose of those containers and clean up the litter.

Several years ago, Dr. Laws prepared a report which compared industry's solution to our burgeoning solid-waste problems, i.e., establishing gigantic materials-recovery systems, to the alternatives of using returnable containers. Her report follows:

> America is choking in its own solid waste. Although it is widely recognized that this problem is due in large measure to the increase in per capita consumption and overpackaging, our response to this problem is depressing but not surprising. Instead of turning off the faucet we choose to mop up the floor. Thus, we are told that

instead of worrying about plastics, throwaway cans and bottles, and the unnecessary paper used in overpackaging, we should develop total solid-waste management systems.

These systems will sort out and process metals, plastics, and glass automatically so that the valuable resources can be recycled

Mandatory-deposit legislation is having a tremendous impact on recycling. Peter Chokola was one of the few bottlers who emphasized returnable bottles while the trend was one-way to throwaways.

and hence saved. The modern solid-waste management system will then incinerate the remaining organic materials, paper and food wastes, in order to generate electrical energy. This procedure is said to be not only good for the environment but good for industry. We are able to keep the container industry alive and healthy and create a whole new technology—solid-waste management.

Needless to say, this manufacture, process, and recycle approach to the solid-waste problem is being advocated strongly by the container industry, the rapidly developing solid-waste management industry, and government agencies which respond to pressures from these industries. Even private citizens have supported this approach by setting up facilities to recycle materials on a volunteer basis. The container manufacturers are happy to explain their role in helping citizen-environmentalists save our national resources by helping to create volunteer recycling centers for cans and bottles.

Let us examine the total environmental impact of the approach to solid waste management outlined above. Since "Earth Day" in 1970, scientists have had time to think, time to start taking an overview, time to begin assessing the environmental impact of various technologies. Three factors are key in determining the environmental impact of a technology:

1. Energy expenditure
2. Depletion of basic raw materials
3. Environmental pollution

Each container-manufacturing process and the corresponding solid-waste management process must be examined separately with these three factors in mind.

The raw materials necessary to manufacture bottles are extremely abundant. Thus pollution and energy depletion are the key factors in assessing the bottle industry. They claim that returning to a returnable beverage-bottle system is unnecessary and would only be a step backward. The additional use of energy to maintain a throwaway-and-recycle system for containers is not mentioned.

In a study of beverage-container systems by Bruce Hannon at

the University of Illinois, the energy required to maintain a throwaway-bottle system and a throwaway-can system was compared to that required to maintain a returnable-bottle system. These energies were computed assuming both processing that involved recycling or landfilling as the final outcome of each type of container system.

The results showed that the worst system for the environment in terms of energy and pollution factors is the system of manufacturing throwaway glass bottles and then recycling them with a current solid-waste management system.

The best system, environmentally, is the old-fashioned returnable-bottle system without recycling at the end. Other systems fall in between in terms of energy requirements.

Bottlers who use an all-returnable system find they can get 24 refills per bottle. Thus by requiring through legislation that all food and drink containers be returnable glass bottles, the volume of cans and bottles in solid waste could be cut to 4 percent of its current volume.

If the 12 billion throwaway beer and soft-drink bottles used in 1970 had been returnable we would have saved at least the equivalent of 13 billion KWH of electrical energy. This is enough to provide residential electrical power to a city of 6½ million relatively affluent residents for one year.

If all food and drink containers were returnable bottles the figure would jump to electrical power for about 20 million residents each year.

Look at this another way, each beverage bottle which we discard instead of returning costs us half a kilowatt-hour—enough energy to burn a 100-watt electric lightbulb for 5 hours.

As Dr. Laws so aptly indicates, the motherhood-and-apple-pie ambience of recycling is shattered by the mandatory-deposit issue. While industry, labor, environmentalist, and Boy Scout alike share an abiding faith in the benefits of recycling resources, all hell breaks loose when it reaches the legislative chambers at the state or federal level.

The major packaging firms and beverage companies release a

stream of statements citing problems with mandatory-deposit experiences. Says a senior vice-president for the American Iron and Steel Institute: "The problems which have developed in Oregon and Vermont following enactment of laws which have effectively banned the use of beverage cans have now become more widely known. In contrast, recycling of cans, and all other kinds of solid waste, is growing rapidly in the U.S." He then noted how the state legislation "badly disrupted" marketing and distribution of beer and soft drinks: "Retailers, supermarkets and soft-drink bottlers faced unprecedented problems. They were hit with substantial costs for labor, storage space for returned bottles, and transportation and processing equipment. Thus, any benefits from ban-the-can legislation are being offset by highly inflationary disadvantages."

"Humbug!" comes back from proponents, who accuse such industry spokesmen of blatant scare tactics, misrepresentation, and downright false propaganda. While there is no doubt that recycling must shift from a voluntary to a mandatory basis, advocates stress that it is inaccurate to refer to the bills as "ban-the-can" or a "bottle bill." Plain and simple, a law like the one in Vermont requires a deposit of at least five cents on each beer and soda container, which is then refunded upon its return.

The Vermont legislature, in an effort to recognize the legitimate concerns of grocers, specified compensation for their handling costs by providing reimbursement from distributors at a rate of a penny for each five-cent container. If a grocer has a particular tactical problem with handling or storage, he usually has the option of having his empties handled by a redemption center. According to the Jeffords–Webster analysis, more than 100 privately operated redemption centers have opened throughout Vermont since enactment of the legislation. Typically, the centers sell beer and soda, as well as providing convenient locations for return of bottles and cans. Beverage sales have not suffered, and grocers report that very few customers bring in large amounts of varied containers for redemption without shopping in the store. "People don't dump bottles on us—99 percent of what we get back are ones we sell, and most people spend their refunds right in the store," one grocer observed.

Some resentment among grocers is noted over the fact that not all of the technically refillable beer bottles are actually being refilled, and not all of the steel cans (as opposed to the aluminum cans) are being recycled. Consequently, strengthening the law to encourage more pervasive reuse and recycling is supported by many grocers. Congressman Jeffords also points out that many Vermonters feel that "while the deposit law makes good sense for Vermont, it would make even better sense on a regional or national scale."

A National Mandatory Deposit on Beverage Containers

Recognizing growing congressional interest in legislating a national mandatory deposit on beverage containers, the General Accounting Office analyzed the effects of such legislation on the environment, the economy, and the consumer, in a report entitled "Potential Effects of a National Mandatory Deposit on Beverage Containers."

Twenty years ago, The GAO statistics show, the average American threw out 75 beverage containers. Today, the amount—a good percentage winding up along roads, lawns, and walkways—has jumped to about 370. Back in 1960, most Americans still purchased their beer and soft drinks in refillable glass bottles which carried a refundable deposit. Now over 70 percent of these beverages are sold in no-deposit glass or metal containers which are used once and discarded. The purpose of a mandatory deposit is to introduce an economic incentive for reusing containers and recycling materials. Proponents maintain that producers and sellers should bear some responsibility for wastes generated, and that the consumer should be more directly aware of the costs of consuming and disposing of one-use packaging.

Opponents of mandatory-deposit legislation contend that manufacturers are only supplying what the consumer wants (convenience), that such cans are only a partial solution, and that it may actually hinder progress since it removes valuable cans from the waste stream which are about to be recovered through municipal recycling programs. Without going into great detail, several points should be made. First, according to a Federal Energy Administration pool, 73 percent of the American public supports a return to refillable bottles. Second, and most important, recovering solid wastes through municipal recycling programs or through resource-recovery programs is costly to the municipality and the taxpayer (to buy the equipment), does not alter wasteful manufacturing and consumption habits, and does not really present a solution to the excess solid-waste problem in general, as the community must still collect and process the beverage containers. Third, while community recycling programs have proven to be successful, the rate of participation and the total return of containers has been low. Having beverage containers with deposits will give consumers a monetary incentive to return the containers. Reports have shown that with a deposit system, 80–90 percent of the beverage containers are returned.

As Charles D. Gassert, vice-president of the Pennsylvania Alliance for Returnables, says: "When U.S. Steel speaks of resource recovery, it is talking about high-technology, capital- and energy-intensive plants paid for and maintained by the taxpayer. U.S. Steel therefore appears to be supporting something good, but its ulterior motive is to avoid any responsibility for reducing or recovering all the energy and raw materials which go into the production of excess packaging."

Effects of Mandatory Deposit on Raw Material Use, Labor, and Energy

The GAO report is especially interesting with regard to the impact of deposit legislation on raw material use—the sand, iron ore, and bauxite used in glass, steel, and aluminum containers.

Iron ore comprises about 55 percent of the material used to make bimetal steel containers and 75 percent of that used to make all-steel cans. Under a mandatory-deposit law, it is predictable that there will be a return to primarily refillable bottles, with cans holding 20 percent of the sales. In that situation, steel-can production in 1985 would drop to 6.6 billion cans from the 39.2 billion forecasted under present trends. The change would reduce iron-ore requirements for the U.S. in 1985 by about 3 million tons, about 2 percent of total iron-ore consumption. Notes the GAO:

> A reduction in iron-ore consumption is important because one-third of U.S. iron ore is now imported, and domestic ore is coming from increasingly lower grade deposits. A decline in the number of steel cans produced and/or an increase in recycling rates would help to extend iron-ore reserves.

Concerning bauxite, the aluminum beverage containers produced in 1975 used about 7 percent of the total U.S. bauxite requirements, or 1.2 million tons. About 25 percent of the 16.6 billion cans produced were estimated to have been recycled. Under projections with a mandatory deposit, there would be a reduction of bauxite use of 1 to 1.4 million tons. "If the potential reductions in raw materials were made mostly from imports," the GAO comments, "there would be important balance of payments trade account benefits."

As would be expected, national legislation would have a

significant impact on the number and weight of containers which now wind up as trash at landfills. By 1985, the way things are going now, some 108 billion containers would be thrown away with the garbage; their weight would be 10.5 million tons. Under a mandatory-deposit system, that figure would drop to 15 to 20 billion containers, weighing somewhere between 2.3 and 3.2 million tons.

The 3.6–4.1 percent potential reduction in the total postconsumer garbage stream is most important, notes the GAO, as landfill and dump sites become scarcer, especially in the urban Northeast where land costs are higher.

The mandatory-deposit bill—local, state, or national—is definitely a piece of legislation that Americans have to adjust to—consumers, industries, labor unions, retailers, and public officials. It is an attempt to slow down and eventually put an end to wasting resources, as well as an attempt to reorient the American public to conserve, reuse, and recycle. Different from the other types of recycling discussed in this book, mandatory-deposit laws directly influence recycling behavior at the consumer level. "A consumer would be able to purchase beverages in any type of container and throw the container away if he or she pleases," explains the GAO. "The consumer who chooses to act in that fashion would lose the deposit, not convenience; convenience would begin to have a definite, attributable cost."

While the opponents of a national mandatory-deposit bill cite the loss of jobs in the beverage-container industries as the most negative factor of the legislation, it appears that out of stubbornness and a desire to ride on the banner of convenience these adversaries ignore the much stronger positive factors. First, the returnable container, especially the refillable bottle, are labor-intensive production processes while the production of throwaway bottles or cans is energy- and material-intensive. A Federal Energy Administration study, as well as GAO and EPA estimates, predicts a net increase of some 117,000 jobs and a net increase in total labor income of nearly $1 billion.

Second, the beverage industries themselves, at least the soda companies, would most likely be able to reduce costs. *Beverage Industry* magazine reported in its January 27, 1978, issue that "U.S. soft drink firms alone will spend the incredible sum of over $4.5 billion on packaging this year." The magazine points out that this $4.5 billion to be spent on packaging materials and supplies represents 82 percent of total planned outlays in 1978.

Third, there will be a very significant decrease in solid waste. A refund which encourages the return of bottles and cans would reduce the weight of our garbage by 7 or 8 million tons annually. If collection costs are currently $30.00 per ton, savings in solid waste costs alone would be around $200 million.

Finally, energy saving would also be significant. According to the Research Triangle Institute study prepared for the FEA, a container-refund measure would reduce national energy consumption by the equivalent of 70,000–81,000 barrels of oil per day.

When you sort through the tremendous amount of literature available on mandatory-deposit legislation, the need emerges for an effective public education program to (1) support passage of such legislation and (2) develop public support for its provisions. While special interests continue to argue vehemently against its passage, such legislation would dramatically reduce litter and arouse public awareness of the issues, significantly cut down the solid-waste flow, save energy, eventually produce more jobs, and offer beverages at a lower cost. Not too bad for a single piece of legislation!

12

Public Policies for Recycling

The importance of such legislation as state and federal mandatory beverage deposits has been described in the previous chapter. Such legislation is by no means all that can be done by elected officials and public agency directors. Besides influencing behavior patterns at the consumer level constructively, other factors also need to be addressed. These factors range from policies for transporting recycled versus virgin materials to creating additional economic incentives for use of recycled fibers.

For example, the market for recycling wastepaper would be much improved if government purchasing departments specified that large percentages of reclaimed fiber be included in their paper supplies. Such precedents already exist, but the practice should be much more commonly used and the minimum percentage level of recycled fiber should be increased.

A number of measures supporting recycling have been listed by various segments of the secondary-materials industry. Such measures include the following:

Transportation Rates: Present costs of transporting recycled

204 ●

materials are sometimes twice as much as for competitive commodities. The secondary-materials dealers urge the Interstate Commerce Commission and state regulatory commissions to implement nondiscriminatory rates on recyclables, rates not to exceed those on competing commodities.

Licensing and Zoning Policies: As resource-recovery concepts replace disposal practices, the process should be treated more like an industrial park than a junkyard and dump. Often locations near urban sources of wastes must be found within local industrial districts. Scrap dealers and recyclers also feel that they should be subjected to the same aesthetic standards and not singled out by special "beautification" laws.

The recycling industry associations give special emphasis to the creation of new incentives, economic and marketing. They seek investment tax credits, similar to pollution-equipment credits, to promote recycling. They would like firms in their associations to receive state income and corporate tax assistance, tax benefits equivalent to those given industries in many states for utilizing virgin materials. Many recycling operations are a manufacturing activity, notes the National Association of Recycling Industries, and the recognition of this status by tax authorities would remove the burden for recyclers of paying sales taxes on the operational equipment they purchase.

Referring to purchasing policies, the NARI takes this position:

> Government purchasing policies—as well as those of industry, boards of education, chambers of commerce, and public institutions—can help create and expand markets for recyclables. Procurement policies and codes should not contain 'virgin only' clauses, and measures should be implemented to maximize the purchase of recycled materials and products wherever and whenever possible.

Some of the NARI's efforts were recently rewarded by congressional approval of an additional 10-percent investment tax

credit for the purchase of equipment used to recycle materials for
. energy conservation. "While the 10-percent investment tax credit in
no way accords the recycling industry parity with virgin material
industries, it is a major step in the right direction," said M. J.
Mighdoll, the NARI's executive vice-president.

An October 1978 NARI press release explains:

> The recycling incentive—the first of its kind in history—provides
> for an additional 10 percent tax credit (for a total of 20 percent) for
> purchases of equipment used to process materials for recycling or
> to actually utilize them in the recycling process through the first-
> product stages, such as the making of metal ingots or paper. The
> credit is applicable to equipment placed in service on October 1,
> 1978, or later. It covers nonferrous metals, paper, textiles, rubber
> and other materials. The credit also applies to iron and steel
> recycling, but it will be applicable only to equipment utilized for
> processing ferrous scrap and not that used in the melting or first-
> product stage of iron and steel scrap recycling.

Also included in the national energy legislation is a recycling-
targets provision "which authorizes the U.S. Department of Energy
to set goals for the nation's major energy-using industries—including
metals, paper, textiles, and rubber—to maximize their use of
recycled materials. Specific targets are to be set for each industry,
calling for projected increases in the use of recycled commodities
over the next ten-year period," reports the NARI.

European countries have adopted or are carefully considering
such policies to improve conditions for recycling. In Denmark, the
government has introduced favorable standards for reclaimed
materials into its public procurement specifications. France has a
similar directive on public organizations using recycled paper, tax
regulations favoring waste oil over primary supplies, and regulations
planned to limit use of certain glues, inks, etc., which inhibit ease of
recycling.

Glass and metal industries in Germany have agreed to use more secondary materials; a 1969 Waste Oil Law provided for subsidies to be awarded for collection and use of waste oil, with the funding coming from a tax on delivered primary supplies. A consortium of British textile reclaimers, set up with government encouragement, has guaranteed to purchase supplies from organized voluntary collections.

The subject of "interjurisdictional contracts" has been cited as an important factor by the National League of Cities and the U.S. Conference of Mayors. Those groups claim that legislation is needed to permit any municipality or other local political jurisdiction to enter into long-term contracts with any individual firm, municipality, state, or the federal government for the purpose of recycling solid wastes. This point is often critical politically, since it deals with the transition of a public liability (waste) into an economic asset (recycled material). As recycling becomes more extensive, the issue must be resolved without constant fanfare.

The group of engineers at the University of California who analyzed the market potential of materials and energy recovered from San Francisco Bay Area solid wastes notes how critical transportation costs of secondary materials are, since in some cases the shipping costs may exceed the value of the material being shipped. They also explained that classification can further confuse the rate-setting issue, i.e., fuel pellets being classed as wastepaper. Factors such as these can contribute to discriminatory freight rates against secondary materials.

According to the University of California study, the Interstate Commerce Act does not explicitly refer to discrimination, although it does make it unlawful for any carrier to give undue or unreasonable advantage to any particular shipper or to subject any shipper to undue or unreasonable prejudice. The case for proving discrimination is difficult, as is evident by these two factors:

1. It must be shown that the rate relationship between

virgin and secondary materials is the source of actual injury to the shippers of secondary materials.

2. Documentation must be provided which demonstrates that current rates for secondary materials are too high relative to rates for virgin materials and as a result there is a decrease in recycling.

With regulations such as these affecting transportation, it's no wonder that the NARI's executive vice-president, M. J. Mighdoll, recently complained:

> It is hard to believe that despite all the lip service given to recycling, there are many state and local laws still being proposed which seriously inhibit the recycling industry's operations and the opportunities to expand recycling to serve the energy, resource, and environmental needs of communities throughout America.

Repealing the Depletion Tax Break

After a two-year study, the National Commission on Supplies and Shortages came up with a conclusion that has been obvious to many people, in or out of the secondary-materials industry. The fraction of materials that comes from recycling has been static or declining, particularly for paper and copper, when it should be increasing.

The commission recommended that Congress repeal the percentage depletion tax break for minerals producers and take other actions to encourage recycling. The 15-percent depletion allowance on taxes paid by minerals producers amounts to a subsidy to use up raw materials, the commission said, and its repeal would amount to an incentive for recycling.

In the University of California market study cited above, researchers under the direction of George Trezek and Clarence Golueke also reviewed national policies which have a direct impact on material usage. They listed factors which would form a basis for the proper allocation of resources and recycling rather than disposal via the waste stream. Besides depletion allowances, stockpiles, and transportation, they also referred to factors of export and import.

Trezek, Golueke, and their colleagues note that various levels of government can have legislative influences on recycling and the resource-recovery industry through some or all of the following factors: pollution codes; export restrictions; depletion allowances; stockpile policy; transportation rates and policy; discriminatory purchasing policies; discriminatory classification, licensing, and restriction of scrap processors; auto-titling laws; zoning laws, etc.

Supreme Court Case Affects Recycling

The 1978 decision of the United States Supreme Court in *City of Philadelphia v. State of New Jersey* will increase the difficulties for a state to isolate itself from regional and national solid-waste disposal problems. In a 7–2 decision, the Supreme Court held that the Commerce Clause of the United States Constitution precluded New Jersey from forbidding the importation for disposal within the state of solid waste originating outside the state.

In an analysis of the decision, attorneys Joseph Manko and Bruce Katcher of Philadelphia explore its implications on encouraging states to adopt recycling legislation, noting that if a state wanted to ban out-of-state wastes in compliance with the Court decision, it could probably enact a recycling law requiring source separation and forbid the disposal of any waste that was not source separated. Thus out-of-state waste would be excluded unless it conformed to source-separation requirements:

> A simple method of excluding out-of-state waste would be the enactment of a "bottle bill" excluding all nonreturnable glass containers. The effect of such a law would, of course, be

dependent on the likelihood that out-of-state waste disposers who wanted to dispose of solid waste in New Jersey would separate out glass containers from the rest of their solid waste.... These laws advance legitimate state interests, i.e., recycling, and therefore seem to meet all the tests set forth in *City of Philadelphia*.

To the extent that states are able and willing to adopt recycling programs, the *City of Philadelphia* case may well have the effect of encouraging such activity, at least if the state is also concerned about excluding out-of-state wastes.

13

Conclusion: A Future Without Dumps

Will all our dumps, at least as we now know them, be closed down in the future? Will the percentage of materials which are recycled increase 5-, 10-, and 20-fold in coming years?

The answers depend on a great many factors:

—the design of products we buy so they have a longer service life
—the use of reclaimed materials in the manufacture of new products
—the vitality of America's conservation ethic

Many trends in our nation encourage a belief that we are ready to travel faster on the road to recycling. Some trends are based on economics: as the costs for disposal go up, the savings in recycling become meaningful. The same goes for higher energy prices. Some trends are legislative: more stringent air- and water-pollution-control laws force industries and cities to salvage wastes *before* discharge. The six states which now have mandatory-deposit legislation may well be establishing the basis for such a law on a national level.

And a most important trend is the shift from enlightened *individual* behavior to broader based *public* policy. One family decides to break the garbage can addiction by separating recyclables and composting; others see how it can be done and adopt similar techniques. One small group begins a grass-roots voluntary recycling project, and soon the city takes it over and makes it official and tax supported.

True, such developments are piecemeal across our nation today—but all the bits and pieces add up to a trend toward recycling. Who knows, maybe even a future without dumps!

Appendix

Suggested Reading List

Barrett, A.; Pyle, L.; and Subramanian, S. K. *Biogas Technology in the Third World.* Ottawa: International Development Research Centre, 1978.

Bendavid-Val. *Starting Your Own Energy Business.* Washington, D.C.: Institute for Local Self-Reliance, 1978.

Bender, Tom. *Living Lightly: Energy Conservation in Housing.* Portland, Oregon: RAIN Publications, 1973.

Bever, Michael; Henstock, B.; and Henstock, Michael E. *Conservation & Recycling.* Oxford: Pergamon Press, Ltd., 1976.

Brown, E. Evan. *World Fish Farming: Cultivation and Economics.* Westport, Conn.: AVI Publishing Co., 1977.

Christensen, L. A.; Connor, L. J.; and Libby, L. W. "An Economic Analysis of the Utilization of Municipal Wastewater for Crop Production." Agricultural Economics Report No. 292. Department of Agricultural Economics. East Lansing, Michigan: Michigan State University, November 1975.

Clark, Robert M. *Analysis of Urban Solid Waste Services—A Systems Approach.* Ann Arbor, Michigan: Ann Arbor Science Publishers, 1978.

Connolly, John A. *Solid Waste Management: Worldwide Solid Waste Literature Collection/Retrieval Services.* EPA SW-636, 1977.

Culp, Gordon L., and Culp, Russell L. *New Concepts in Water Purification.* New York: Van Nostrand Reinhold Environmental Engineering Series, 1974.

Devik, O. (ed.). *Harvesting Polluted Waters.* New York: Plenum Press, 1976.

Goldman, M. I. *Ecology and Economics—Controlling Pollution in the '70's.* Englewood Cliffs, N.J.: Prentice-Hall, 1972.

Goldstein, Jerome. *Sensible Sludge.* Emmaus, Penna.: Rodale Press, 1976.

Golueke, Clarence G. *Composting: A Study of the Process and Its Principles.* Emmaus, Penna.: Rodale Press, 1972.

———.*Biological Reclamation of Solid Waste.* Emmaus, Penna.: Rodale Press, 1977.

Hagerty, D. Joseph; Pavoni, Joseph L.; and Heer, John E., Jr. *Solid Waste Management.* New York: Van Nostrand Reinhold Environmental Engineering Series, 1973.

Hartenstein, Roy (ed.). *Utilization of Soil Organisms in Sludge Management.* Syracuse: SUNY College of Forestry, 1978.

Hayes, Denis. *Repairs, Reuse, Recycling—Moving Towards a Sustainable Society.* Worldwatch Paper 23. Washington, D.C.: Worldwatch Institute, 1978.

Henderson, H. *Creating Alternative Futures.* New York: Berkeley Publishing, 1978.

House, David. *The Complete Bio Gas Handbook.* Aurora, Oregon: At Home Everywhere, 1978.

Inglett, George E. (ed.). *Symposium: Processing Agricultural and Municipal Wastes.* Westport, Conn.: AVI Publishing Co., 1973.

Jacobs, Lee W. (ed.). *Utilizing Municipal Sewage Wastewaters and Sludges on Land for Agricultural Production.* Michigan: Michigan State Univ., 1977.

Jeffords, James M. (Congressman-Vt.) and Donald W. Webster (Director of Environmental Protection-Vt.). *Vermont 5¢ Deposit.* Preliminary Edition, November, 1977.

Jewell, William J. (ed.). *Energy, Agriculture and Waste Management.* Ann Arbor, Mich.: Ann Arbor Science Publishers, 1975.

Loehr, Raymond C. (ed.). *Land as a Waste Management Alternative.* Ann Arbor, Mich.: Ann Arbor Science Publishers, 1977.

McClelland, Nina I. (ed.). *Individual Onsite Wastewater Systems.* Ann Arbor, Mich.: Ann Arbor Science Publishers, 1978.

McCullagh, James C. (ed.). *Ways to Play—Recreation Alternatives.* Emmaus, Penna.: Rodale Press, 1978.

McGarry, Michael E., and Stainforth, Jill (eds.). *Compost Fertilizer and Biogas Production from Human and Farm Wastes in the People's Republic of China.* Ottawa: International Development Research Centre, 1978.

Meynell, Peter-John. *Methane: Planning a Digester.* New York: Schocken Books, 1976.

Morse, Alex; Bhatt, Vikram; and Rybczynski, Witold. *Water Conservation and the Mist Experience.* Montreal: Minimum Cost Housing Group, McGill Univ., 1978.

Nesius, E. J., and Thung, Bui Cong. *Solid Waste Management for Rural Areas: An Annotated Bibliography.* West Virginia: West Virginia Division of Resource Management, 1977.

Olsen, Christine (ed.). *Recycling: The State of the Art.* Santa Barbara, Calif.: Community Environmental Council, 1976.

"Oregon's Bottle Bill: The 1977 Report." State of Oregon Department of Environmental Quality. Portland, Oregon: Recycling Information Office, 1977.

Pavoni, Joseph L.; Herr, John E., Jr.; and Hagerty, D. Joseph. *Handbook of Solid Waste Disposal: Materials and Energy Recovery.* New York: Van Nostrand Reinhold Environmental Engineering Series, 1975.

Perry, Stewart E. *San Francisco Scavengers.* Berkeley: University of California Press, 1978.

Poincelot, Raymond P. *The Biochemistry and Methodology of Composting.* Bulletin 754. New Haven: The Connecticut Agricultural Experiment Station, September 1975.

Rodale, J. I., and Staff. *The Complete Book of Composting.* Emmaus, Penna.: Rodale Books, 1971.

Stoner, Carol Hupping. *Goodbye to the Flush Toilet.* Emmaus, Penna.: Rodale Press, 1977.

Tarr, Joel A. "From City to Farm: Urban Wastes and the American Farmer." *Agricultural History* (October 1975).

Tchobanoglous, H.; Thiesen, H.; and Eliassen, R. *Solid Wastes—Engineering Principles and Management Issues.* New York: McGraw-Hill, 1977.

Theios, Joyce (ed.). *Composting Toilets.* Oregon: Lane County Office of Appropriate Technology, 1978.

Trezek, G. J. "Significance of Size Reduction in Solid Waste Management." Report prepared for the Solid and Hazardous Waste Research Division, Municipal Environmental Resource Lab., U.S. EPA, Cincinnati, Ohio 45268, July 1977.

Van der Ryn, Sim. *The Toilet Papers—Designs to Recycle Human Waste and Water: Dry Toilets, Greywater Systems & Urban Sewage.* Santa Barbara, Calif.: Capra Press, 1978.
Wilson, David Gordon (ed.). *Handbook of Solid Waste Management.* New York: Van Nostrand Reinhold, 1977.

"Bioconversion." Washington, D.C.: Citizens' Energy Project Publications, 1978.
Compost—An Annotated Bibliography on Compost, Compost Quality and Composting (1971-1977). Duebendorf, Switzerland: WHO International Reference Center for Wastes Disposal, 1978.
Composting of Municipal Solid Wastes in the United States. Solid Waste Management Series SW-47r. Washington, D.C.: U.S. Environmental Protection Agency, 1971.
Composting Sewage Sludge—From Waste to Resource. U.S. Department of Agriculture, Agricultural Research Service and Maryland Environmental Service, September 1973.
Disposal of Residues on Land. Proceedings of National Conference on Disposal of Residues on Land (Sept. 1976). Rockville, Md.: Information Transfer, Inc., 1977.
"How to Recycle Wasterpaper." The Paper Stock Conservation Committee. New York: The American Paper Institute, 1978.
Land Application of Thermally Treated Sewage Sludge. Technical Bulletin 2250-T. Rothschild, Wisconsin: Zimpro, Inc., 1978.
Methane Generation From Human, Animal and Agricultural Wastes. Washington, D.C.: National Academy of Sciences, 1977.
Potential Effects of a National Mandatory Deposit on Beverage Containers. Report to the Congress by the Comptroller General of the U.S., Dec. 7, 1977.
Proceedings: Waste Management Technology and Resource & Energy Recovery. SW-8p. Co-sponsored by U.S. EPA and the National Solid Wastes Management Assn., November 1975. Washington, D.C.: U.S. Environmental Protection Agency, 1976.
Process Design Manual for Sludge Treatment and Disposal. Washington, D.C.: U.S. Environmental Protection Agency, October 1974.
RAINBOOK: Resources for Appropriate Technology. Portland, Ore.: Schocken Books, 1977.

"Recycling in Your Community." New York: National Association of Recycling Industries, 1978.

Recycling Municipal Sludges and Effluents on Land. Proceedings of Joint Conference sponsored by the Environmental Protection Agency, U.S. Department of Agriculture, and National Association of State Universities and Land-Grant Colleges, July 9–13, 1973.

"Recycling Responds." National Association of Recycling Industries. New York, 1978.

The Strip Mine Handbook. Center for Law & Social Policy. Washington, D.C.: Environmental Policy Institute, 1978.

"Turning Trash Into Cash: How You Can Get Action on Resource Recovery in Your Community." Pittsburgh, Penna.: United States Steel, 1978.

"Waste Not, Want Not." Minnesota Pollution Control Agency. Roseville, Minn., 1978.

Associations and Publications

Adolph Coors Company
Public Relations Dept. 802
Golden, CO 80401
  Alumninews (monthly)

• Alternative Waste Management
  Assn.
Box 32240
Calvert Street Station
Washington, DC 20007

American Can Company
American Lane
Greenwich, CT 06830
  Resource Recovery

American Paper Institute
260 Madison Avenue
New York, NY 10016

Crusade for a Cleaner Environment
2000 L Street NW, Suite 520
Washington, DC 20036

National Association of Recycling, Inc.
330 Madison Avenue
New York, NY 10017

National Clearinghouse on Deposit
  Legislation
Environmental Action Foundation
724 Dupont Circle Building
Washington, DC 20036

Pennsylvania Alliance for
  Returnables, Inc.
Box 472 Federal Square Station
Harrisburg, PA 17108
  P.A.R. Progress Report
    (bimonthly)

Steel Products News Bureau
633 Third Avenue
New York, NY 10017

Alternative Sources of Energy
Rt. 2
Milaca, MN 56353
    U.S. (bimonthly)

Compost Science/Land Utilization
Journal of Waste Recycling
Box 351
Emmaus, PA 18049

Institute for Rural Sanitation
    Services (IRSS)
National Demonstration Water
    Project (NDWP)
1820 Jefferson Place NW
Washington, DC 20036

• National Center for Resource
    Recovery, Inc.
1211 Connecticut Avenue NW
Washington, DC 20036
    NCRR Update (monthly)

*RAIN—Journal of Appropriate
    Technology*
2270 NW Irving
Portland, OR 97210

Self-Reliance
Institute for Local Self-Reliance
1717 18th Street NW
Washington, DC 20009

Water & Wastes Digest
Scranton Gillette Communications,
    Inc.
434 S. Wabash Avenue
Chicago, IL 60605

World Association for Solid Waste
    Transfer and Exchange (WASTE)
152 Utah Avenue
S. San Francisco, CA 94080

Garden Compost Shredders

Allis-Chalmers
Outdoors Leisure Products Div.
1126 S. 70th POB 512
Milwaukee, WI 53201

Amerind-MacKissic
Box 111
Parker Ford, PA 19457

Ariens
111 Calumet & 655 W. Ryan St.
Brillion, WI 54110

Atlas Tool & Mfg. Co.
5151 Natural Bridge Ave.
St. Louis, MO 63115

Bolens Div. FMC Corp.
Urban/Suburban Power Equip.
  Div.
215 S. Park St.
Port Washington, WI 53074

Columbia
PO Box 2741, 5389 W. 130th St.
Cleveland, OH 44111

Gilson Brothers Mfg. Co.
Box 152
Plymouth, WI 53073

Hahn, Inc. Agricultural Products
  Div.
1625 N. Garvin St.
Evansville, IN 47717

International Harvester
401 N. Michigan Avenue
Chicago, IL 60611

Jacobsen Mfg. Co.
1721 Packard Avenue
Racine, WI 53403

F.D. Kees Mfg. Co.
Box 775, 700 Park Ave.
Beatric, NB 68310

Lindig Mfg. Corp.
Box 111, 1877 W. County Rd. C.
St. Paul, MN 55113

Magna American Corp.
Box 90, Hwy. 18
Raymond, MS 39150

McDonough Power Equipment,
  Inc.
Macon Road
McDonough, GA 30253

MTD Products, Inc.
Box 2741, 5389 W. 130th
Cleveland, OH 44111

Red Cross Mfg. Corp.
Box 111, 124 S. Oak
Bluffton, IN 46714

Roof Mfg. Co.
1011 W. Howard St.
Pontiac, IL 61764

Roper Sales Corp.
1905 W. Court St.
Kankakee, IL 60901

Roto-Hoe & Sprayer Co.
100 Auburn Road, Rt. 87
Newbury, OH 44065

Sears, Roebuck & Co.
925 S. Homan Avenue
Chicago, IL 60607

Toro Co.
8111 Lyndale Avenue S
Bloomington, MN 55420

Winona Attrition Mill
1009 W. Fifth Street
Winona, MN 55987

Directory of Composting Systems

The increasing interest in composting by both municipalities and industry has provided an excellent opportunity for many businesses to enter this field with needed products. Because of the wide range of composting techniques in use, many varieties of equipment and services are in demand.

Several companies market complete composting systems—from shredders at the front end of the operation to screens and baggers at the back end. Other companies sell only one or two components needed in a composting system. Still others presently concern themselves only with shredding systems.

Listed below are American and European firms which include composting or shredding equipment among their products. Many more companies manufacture hardware applicable to composting technology than can be mentioned here. However, most of the major commercial enterprises in this field are found listed below:

AENCO, Inc.
1502 Reybold Ave., P.O. Box 387
New Castle, DE 19720

Contact: Anthony Nollet
      (302) 328-1361

Composting, Shredding, and Reclamation System: Produces humus; controls pathogens; eliminates toxic leachate; extends landfill life; reclaims ferrous scrap; minimizes odor and vermin problems.

Penn Green "Big Job" Composter: Windrow turner; one-man operation; self-feeder; capacity, 600 tons or 1,000 cubic yards per day; powered by gasoline, diesel, or LP gas; four-wheel drive.

Allis Chalmers, Inc.
Solid Waste Processing
3033 West Spencer St.
Appleton, WI 54911

Contact: Robert Brickner
      (414) 734-9831

Large-Capacity Shredder System: Complete line of shredders; hard-faced hammermills; deflector grating for secondary sizing; reinforced heavy duty frame; replaceable wear liners; fogging spray for dust control; explosion suppression system.

American Pulverizer Company
1249 Macklind Ave. 5540 West Park
St. Louis, MO 63110

Contact: Don Graveman
(314) 781-6100

Oversized Bulky Waste Shredder: Composting capability using a two-stage system; can be run in either direction without changing hammers; powered by 1,000-hp motor; reduces waste to fist size.

Arus-Ruthner of America Corp.
404 Carlton House
Pittsburgh, PA 15219

Contact: Harold Bauer
(412) 562-0444

Parent Company:
Ruthner Industrieanlagen Aktiengesellschaft
A-1121 Vienna, Aichholzgasse 51-53
Austria

Refuse Composting Plants: Ruthner MSA System; refuse-sludge-aeration process; separation of ferrous and nonferrous metals, glass, and plastics; high degree of pathogen kill; rapid fermentation process in slowly rotating drums; ripening of compost on aerated plate.

The Black Clawson Company
Shartle/Pandia Division
Middletown, OH 45042

Contact: Paul Marsh
(513) 422-4561

Hydrasposal System: Composting capability; separation of glass, sand, and metals; salvage of usable fibers; total recycling, zero-pollution system.

Buhler-Miag, Inc.
1100 Xenium Lane, P.O. Box 9497
Minneapolis, MN 55440

Contact: Wolf Ebert
      (612) 545-1401

Parent Company:
Buhler Brothers Ltd.
Dept. UT
CH9240 Uzwil
Switzerland

Refuse and Sewage-Sludge Recycling Plants: Refuse processing and size
   reduction; automatic fermentation into compost; treatment of compost
   into a variety of grades; ferrous and glass recovery; custom-designed.

Compro-STAR 4000: Windrow turner; homogenizes and aerates windrows;
   can be equipped with automatic controls.

Canadian Bioreactors/American Bioreactor Corp.
P.O. Box 280
Scotstown, Quebec JOB 3BO
Canada

Contact: R. D. Wright
      (819) 657-4924

Parent Company:
BAV Biologische Abfallverwertungsges. GmbH
Berliner Str. 22
6369 Schoneck 1
West Germany

Bioreactor (Kneer System): Converts sludge and solid wastes into compost;
   forced incubation and aeration process; pathogen destruction; two-week
   process; screened out residues suitable for clean landfill operations.

Dambach-Industrieanlagen GmbH
Adolf-Dambach-Str.
7560 Gaggenau
West Germany

Contact: VT/Dr. Vogel
      (07225) 64-288

Bio-Cell-Reactor (System Schnorr): Chambered tower with aeration holes; shredding, screening and ferrous separation pretreatment; 14–28-day composting process; complete pathogen destruction.

Fairfield Service Company
P.O. Box 354
Marion, OH 43302

Contact: Jim Coulson
(614) 387-3335

Fairfield Digester: Designed to receive unsegregated municipal solid waste with or without sewage sludge; continuous-flow automatically controlled aerobic-thermophilic process; pathogen destruction and weed seed sterilization; further processed into a marketable humus product.

Dano Resource Recovery, Inc.
713 N. Fayette St., Suite 201
Alexandria, VA 22314

Contact: Dorothy J. South
(703) 549-7010

Parent Company:
Vereinigte Kesselwerke Aktiengesellschaft
Postfach 8240
D-4000 Dusseldorf 1
West Germany

Refuse Composting Plants: Continuous and fully mechanized biological system; combination sewage-sludge and solid-waste composting capability; industrially valuable materials can be recovered for reuse.

Detroit Stoker Company
1510 East 1st St.
Monroe, MI 48161

Contact: Jim Hall
(313) 241-9500

Detroit Crusher-Shredder: Complete line of shredders; horizontal feed and shredding design; discharge sizing grid; continuous feed of extra-long items possible; particle size reduction ideal for use as fuel.

Enterprise Company
616 South Sante Fe
Santa Ana, CA 92705

Contact: John Kossakoski
(714) 835-0541

Enterprise Shredders: Part of a complete resource recovery system; reduces particle size to minus five inches; dual-rotor design; spiral patterned, hard-faced hammers; spring-loaded chute rejects trap material.

Flakt, Inc.
1500 East Putnam Ave.
Old Greenwich, CT 06870

Contact: Stewart Marshall
(203) 637-5401

Parent Company:
AB Svenska Flaktfabricken
Fack, S-104 60 Stockholm
Sweden

RRR System: Resources recovery from refuse; separation of ferrous metals, aluminum, other metals, glass, plastics, paper fiber, and organics; dry system using air-classification principles.

Fratelli Ingg. Ferrero
Officine Maccaniche
17047 Vado Ligure
Via Privata Trento, 4
Cas.P. 60 Italy

Contact: Marco Pellifroni
(019) 881951

Composting Plants (Ferrero System): Solid wastes milled with glass, plastics, rubber, and wood separated out; remainder composted with mixture of sewage sludge; finished compost is hygienated and homogenized.

Gruendler Crusher and Pulverizer Company
2915 North Market St.
St. Louis, MO 63106

Contact: Mike Kerper
(314) 531-1220

Leaf Shredder: Reduces leaf volume by 17 to 1; prepares leaves for mulch or composting; vacuum intake; gasoline or diesel powered; shreds from 25 to 250 cubic yards per hour.

Primary Refuse Shredder: Hammermills made of chrome-manganese alloy; all-steel frame; 800 to 1200 hp.

Hammermills, Inc.
625 C Avenue NW
Cedar Rapids, IA 52405

Contact: Dave Green
(319) 365-0441

Bulldog Refuse Shredders: Full range of sizes; staggered long-short, full-swing, reversible hammers; patented, reversible, shear-action cutter bar; massive high-inertia steel rotor; electric, diesel, or steam turbine drive.

The Heil Company
300 West Montana Street
Milwaukee, WI 53201

Contact: Paul Miller
(414) 647-3333

Heil Shredders: Municipal, commercial, and industrial applications; dual rotation on hammers for long life; large, nonshreddable objects are ballistically rejected; up to 80 tons per hour capacity.

Hazemag USA, Inc.
P.O. Box 15515
Pittsburgh, PA 15244

Contact: Chris Martin
(412) 787-7711

Parent Company:
Hazemag GmbH
Postfach 3447
4400 Muenster-Westfalen
West Germany

Garbage Composting Plants: Primary shredding unit; fermentation towers and windrow area; sewage sludge can be added; noncompostables are incinerated; impact mixing; compost ready in 3–6 months.

Industrie-Werke Karlsruhe Augsburg Aktiengesellschaft
Postfach 3409
7500 Karlsruhe 1
West Germany

Contact: H. Schriewer
(0721) 143-036

Composting Plant (Brikollare System): Combination sewage-sludge and solid-waste composting; hydraulically compressed mixture of wastes composts aerobically without mechanical devices; total pathogen kill and substantial dehumidification.

Jeffrey Manufacturing Co.
Division of Dresser Industries, Inc.
P.O. Box 2252
Columbus,OH

Contact: R. D. Prushing
(614) 438-3432

Shredders: Complete line of shredders; ability to shred wood and bark, rubber, plastic, and paper fiber; rolled plate and structural-steel frame; heavy-duty rotor mounted on steel-alloy shaft; variety of steel-alloy hammers.

Koppers, Inc.
Sprout-Waldron Division
Waste Processing Dept.
Muncy, PA 17756

Contact: K. A. Sterrett
(717) 546-8211

Components for Aerated Pile Composting Systems: An assortment of equipment including double-agitated mixers. Trommel screens, material-handling systems, storage bins and blower fans.

Lindig Manufacturing Corp.
1875 West County Road C
St. Paul, MN 55113

Contact: John Lindig
   (612) 633-3072

Screens: Ability to screen compost, sludge, wood chips, topsoil, among other materials; rubber-paddle feeder; cleaning brush assembly; provides important aeration, mixing, and texture control of finished sludge compost; shredder attachment reduces compost compaction.

Mehlaf Machine and Manufacturing Co.
Hwy 81, Box 523
Freeman, SD 57029

Contact: Charles Mehlaf
   (605) 925-4512

Easy Over Compost Turner: Capable of turning 400–500 tons per hour; tractor driven; straddles pile 12 foot wide, 4 foot high; mounted on a three-point hitch; leaves peaked row; shreds and aerates as it turns material; reasonably priced.

Newell Manufacturing Co.
P.O. Box 9367
San Antonio, TX 78204

Contact: Jerry Bench
   (512) 227-3141

Solid Waste Shredders: Reclaims metals, glass, and sand; prewired modulated control center; hammer mill made of high-impact steel; air-separation unit removes contaminants by weight; 1,000–4,000 hp; 15–60 tons per day capacity.

Organic Recycling, Inc.
967 South Matlack Street
West Chester, PA 19380

Contact: Jonathan Ponter
(215) 436-6070

The Organo-System: Two-stage process; toroidal dryer dries and classifies
sludge; finished product can be compacted, granulated, and pelletized
for easy shipping; pollution-control system; modular for convenient
expansion.

Pennsylvania Crusher Corp.
P.O. Box 100
Broomall, PA 19008

Contact: John Bradley
(215) 544-7200

Solid Waste Shredders: Bulky-waste, heavy-duty, and industrial-type
shredders; capacity ranges to over 100 tons per hour; custom designed;
end product size of ½ inch or less; may be used in series.

Resource Conversion Systems, Inc.
9039 Katy Freeway, Suite 300
Houston, TX 77024

Contact: Nugent Myrick
(713) 461-9228

Metro-Waste Composting System: System to compost and dewater municipal and industrial organic sludges; fully automated; mechanically reliable;
continuous process control; requires a minimum of operating personnel;
enclosed for all-weather operation.

Roscoe Brown Corporation
P.O. Box 48
Lenox, IA 50851

Contact: Stan Brown
(515) 333-4353

Brown Bear Auger: Windrow turner; replaceable edges on auger permit multi-uses; variable speed; hydrostatic driven; turns 3,000 cubic yards per hour, 50 tons per minute; energy efficient; 142-225 hp; also capable of backfilling, blending, scarifying, and moving ice and snow.

Royer Foundry & Machine Co.
P.O. Box 1232
Kingston, PA 18704

Contact: Charles Otto
     (717) 287-9624

Royer Sludge Shredder: Processes composted or digested sludge into a useful soil conditioner; shreds, cleans, and aerates; 125 cubic yard per hour capacity; all-hydraulic; diesel powered; smaller sizes available.

Sweco, Inc.
6033 East Bandini Boulevard
P.O. Box 4151
Los Angeles, CA 90051

Contact: Robert Kenagy
     (213) 726-1177

Vibro-Energy Separators: Screening system for compost containing a bulking agent; complete line; single or multiple separations; no transmitted vibration; few moving parts; little maintenance required; three-phase, 1,200-rpm motor.

Tracor-Marksman, Inc.
6500 Tracor Lane
Austin, TX 78721

Contact: Fred Burgess
     (512) 926-6658

Shredding and Ferrous Recovery Systems: Horizontal shaft hammermill; wound-rotor main-drive motor; Dings magnet for ferrous recovery; 50-200 tons per hour capacity; completely compatible with an energy recovery system.

United Farm Tools, Inc.
Miller Division
P.O. Box 336
Turlock, CA 95380

Contact: Richard Veeck
(209) 632-3846

Multi-Master Mills: Triple impact action; replaceable wear plates; built of ½-inch steel plate; hardfaced swing hammers; screening system for separation; 20–150 hp.

W-W Grinder Corp.
2957 N. Market St.
Wichita, KS 67219

Contact: Jim Hadley
(316) 838-4229

W-W Hammermills: Tungsten-carbide-tipped hammers; gray cast-iron frame; wide feed opening; interchangeable screens; magnetic separator; special garbage-grinding option; low horsepower requirements.

Williams Patent Crusher & Pulverizer Co.
2701 North Broadway
St. Louis, MO 63102

Contact: Joan Stoeklin
(314) 621-3348

Municipal Solid Waste Shredders: Complete line of shredders; material reduced to a nominal two inches; air classifiers and magnetic separators; glass and aluminum removal process; 80 tons per hour capacity; 1,000-hp, 900-rpm electric motor.

Organic Processing Systems, Inc.
1222 East 26th Street
Erie, PA 16504

Contact: John Bartone
(814) 456-0089

OPS Plants: Accepts organics ranging from wood chippings and leaves to shrub and grass clippings to garbage and sewage sludge; shredding unit available to texturize the end product.

Resource Recovery Systems of Nebraska, Inc.
Route 4
Sterling, CO 80751

Contact: Les Kuhlman
        (303) 522-0663

Scarab: Windrow turner; flails, aerates, and fluffs organic wastes; straddles 14-foot-wide pile; capable of turning up to 1,500 tons of organic wastes per hour; diesel powered; hydrostatic drive.

Voest-Alpine
Vereinigte Oesterreichische Eisen-und-Stahlwerke
Alpine Montan AG
A-4010 Linz, Postfach 2
Austria

Contact: J. Gruber
        (0732) 585

Composting Plants: Fast rotting method; capable of processing both refuse and sewage sludge; bulky-refuse shredding system; iron separation; dual rotting cycles; completely mature compost after 3–4 months.

Von Roll AG
Zurich, Switzerland

Composting Plants (Willisch Process): Hygienically treats waste matter for reuse; ability to sort out glass and metals; sewage sludge may be added; can reduce grain size to 15 mm; output 10–300 tons per hour.

Cobey Composter
Division of Eagle Crusher Co., Inc.
4250 S.R. 309
Galion, OH 44833

Contact: Herbert Cobey
(419) 468-2288

Cobey Composter: Windrow turner; can be used inside or outside; diesel powered; self-propelled; hydrostatic drive; patented drum-mounted teeth chew and aerate material; flotation tires; ability to turn within half its own width.

Mitts & Merrill
109 McCoskry St.
Saginaw, MI 48601

Contact: (517) 752-6191

Mitts & Merrill Shredder: Effectively shreds wood, metal, containers of steel, aluminum and glass, tires and paper; no cutting action, uses hooks to tear and rip; asynchronous counterrotation; low-speed, high-torque shaft rotation; axial play control.

Consultants in the Land Treatment and Composting Fields

W. J. Bauer, Inc.
20 North Wacker Drive
Chicago, IL 60606

Betz-Converse-Murdoch, Inc.
Plymouth Meeting, PA 19462

Boyle Engineering Corporation
1501 Quail St.
P.O. Box 3030
Newport Beach, CA 92663

Brown and Caldwell Consulting Engineers
1501 N. Broadway
Walnut Creek, CA 94596

Buck, Seifert & Jost, Inc.
140 Sylvan Ave.
Englewood Cliffs, NJ 07632

Cal Recovery Systems, Inc.
160 Broadway, Suite 200
Richmond, CA 94804

Camp Dresser & McKee, Inc.
One Center Plaza
Boston, MA 02108

Consoer, Townsend & Associates,
Ltd.
360 East Grand Ave.
Chicago, IL 60611

Engineering Enterprises, Inc.
Norman, Oklahoma

Bird and Hale, Ltd.
Toronto, Canada

Environmental Technology
Consultants, Inc.
6501 Loisdale Court, Suite 502
Springfield, VA 22150

Greeley and Hansen
222 South Riverside Plaza
Chicago, IL 60606

Hoyle and Tanner
Manchester, New Hampshire

Golden Plains Construction
P.O. Box 420
Yuma, CO 80759

Pio Lombardo & Associates
90 Canal St.
Boston, MA 02114

Energy Resources Company
185 Alewife Brook Parkway
Cambridge, MA 02138

Lester Haug
Private Consultant
Los Angeles, California

Alexander Potter Associates
One World Trade Center, Suite 2637
New York, NY 10048

Resource Conservation Consultants
1615 N.W. 23rd Ave., Suite One
Portland, OR 97210

Shaeffer & Roland, Inc.
20 North Wacker Drive
Chicago, IL 60606

Snell Environmental Group
1120 May St.
Lansing, MI 48906

Technological Resources, Inc.
Campbell Place
Camden, NJ 08101

Wehrman Engineering
Middletown, New York

Vermicomposting Consultants and Researchers

Arete Vermicomp Corporation
P.O. Box 426
Dalton, OH 44618

California Vermiculture Exchange
P.O. Box 3058
Santa Rosa, CA 95402

Collier Worm Ranch
2022 Cabrillo St.
Santa Clara, CA 95051

Dan Dindal
SUNY—College of Environmental
Science & Forestry
Syracuse, NY 13210

Ecology International, Inc.
8652 Magnolia Ave., Suite 37
Santee, CA 92071

Roy Hartenstein
SUNY College of Environmental
Science & Forestry
Syracuse, NY 13210

Planet Earthworms
Box 418
Boulder, CO 80302

Nellie Stark
Dept. of Forestry
University of Montana
Missoula, MT 59801

PERIODICALS

The Vermiculture Journal
8652 Magnolia Ave., Suite 37
Santee, CA 92071

World Wide Vermiculture, Inc.
(NEWS)
P.O. Box 4353
Montgomery, AL 36101

Worm Magazine
Northeast 3rd St.
Ridgefield, WA 98642

Index